Praise for *Easy Tarot Reading*

A truly unique book, *Easy Tarot Reading* allows us to experience and understand the mysteries of the tarot. Ellershaw lifts the veil on what it is like to be a professional Tarot reader. She transports us inside the reading room, where she shares the readings and stories of real peo-ple with various backgrounds. This engaging and honest behind-the-scenes glimpse into the world of Tarot will delight and inspire both Tarot enthusiasts and curious newcomers alike.

—Lisa Finander, author of *Disneystrology*

EASY TAROT
READING

Photo by: www.rightclickstudios.com

About the Author

For Josephine Ellershaw, the Tarot has been a constant life companion on a personal journey that spans more than three decades. Alongside her business background she has many years of experience providing readings, healing, and metaphysical guidance to an international clientele. She is also the author of *Easy Tarot: Learn to Read the Cards Once and For All!*

Josie lives in North Yorkshire, England, with her family and a large menagerie of pets, including waifs, strays, and rescues. She always appreciates hearing from readers sharing their experiences and enjoyment of her books, so please visit her website: **www.JosephineEllershaw.com**

To Write to the Author

If you wish to contact the author or would like more information about this book, please write to the author in care of Llewellyn Worldwide, and we will forward your request. Both the author and publisher appreciate hearing from you and learning of your enjoyment of this book and how it has helped you. Llewellyn Worldwide cannot guarantee that every letter written to the author can be answered, but all will be forwarded. Please write to:

Josephine Ellershaw
℅ Llewellyn Worldwide
2143 Wooddale Drive
Woodbury, MN 55125-2989

Please enclose a self-addressed stamped envelope for reply,
or $1.00 to cover costs. If outside the USA, enclose
an international postal reply coupon.

EASY TAROT
READING

THE PROCESS REVEALED IN
TEN TRUE READINGS

Josephine Ellershaw
Author of the Bestselling *Easy Tarot*

Llewellyn Publications
Woodbury, Minnesota

FIRST EDITION
First Printing, 2011

Book design by Bob Gaul
Cover art © 2011 Ciro Marchetti
Cover design by Ellen Lawson
Interior sun art from *Art Explosion Image Library Catalog* (Nova Development Corporation, 2004),
 Tarot card spreads and key © Llewellyn Art Department

Llewellyn is a registered trademark of Llewellyn Worldwide Ltd.

Library of Congress Cataloging-in-Publication Data
Ellershaw, Josephine.
 Easy tarot reading : the process revealed in ten true readings / Josephine Ellershaw. — 1st ed.
   p. cm.
 Includes bibliographical references.
 ISBN 978-0-7387-2137-8
 1. Tarot. I. Title.
 BF1879.T2E475 2011
 133.3'2424—dc23
                          2011023513

Llewellyn Publications
A Division of Llewellyn Worldwide Ltd.
2143 Wooddale Drive
Woodbury, MN 55125-2989
www.llewellyn.com

Printed in the United States of America

Dedication

For my mother, Daphne.
The Queen of Wands
who kept my world turning
whilst I wrote.

Contents

Appendix A   215

Foreword for *Easy Tarot Reading*

Josephine Ellershaw, through her book *Easy Tarot*, has introduced tens of thousands of people in three languages to the joys of Tarot. Her clear writing style coupled with her years of reading experience give the beginning tarot reader the perfect foundation for their tarot practice.

After studying *Easy Tarot*, Josephine's fans and students were quickly reading the cards for themselves. But they were soon ready for the next step and wanted to take their readings to the next level. There is a huge step from understanding what the cards mean to weaving everything together to create a coherent message.

Actually, readers in general, not just Josephine's fans, have been clamoring for a book like this for as long as I've been acquiring Tarot—more than ten years now. I've asked other authors to take on this challenge. Most refused—for how do you teach something as layered and complex, such an intricate combination of skills and intuition?

Josephine bravely took on this task; and in fact, she offered to do so, at the request of her many readers and fans. I am awed when I imagine the amount of work she put into this book. You will see and be amazed, too. She covers every reading in clear, brilliant detail. In addition, she had each client follow up for months after the reading. The information gained through this undertaking is priceless. Reading this book is like being in the mind of a master Tarot reader, which, in a way, you are. Only it seems much clearer and more organized than one would expect.

If, after reading this book, your readings do not improve by leaps and bounds, you must not have been paying attention. Although the book is called *Easy Tarot Reading*, there is something here for all of us, no matter our experience level.

Josephine, thank you for taking on this task, for going where angels and even Fools fear to tread. You deserve multitudes of praise and many thanks, which I know will come your way. But I think I am first: Well done, very well done! And thank you.

Barbara Moore
October 2010

Introduction

*T*ake ten people, add a Tarot reading, blend in their uniquely varied worlds, and the resulting stories produced a far more potent alchemy than originally anticipated. The book developed a direction of its own, powered by the actual life events of those who featured in the readings. We followed their journey, sharing their innermost hopes, fears, plans, ambitions, challenges, and success they encountered along the way. My initial trepidation was replaced as I found myself immersed within the suspense of their unfolding stories.

This book was written in direct response to requests from *Easy Tarot* readers as they made the transition to reading for others. As a teaching tool the most logical route seemed to be to record some actual readings, since it was the most realistic way to demonstrate the cards in action. Taking it a step further, I decided to follow the progress of our subjects, to provide us with a complete picture of the reading, before, during, and after their visit. What I had not bargained for was the nerve-racking yet exhilarating journey that followed. The praise deserving here is to those people who so honestly and generously opened their personal lives to us, for without their participation this book would not have been possible. I know they will fully appreciate my humour, imparted lovingly, when I inform you that at times it felt like herding cats as I attempted to follow their progress!

The Tarot silently beavered away, astounding as always in their mysterious way, the evidence of their wisdom sometimes only fully apparent in the final conclusion of those readings. Meanwhile, my role was like a bridge between the Tarot and the seeker, relaying the messages and keeper of words for your reference. As I set off down this road I began to question myself,

I vowed it must have been some terrible misjudgement on my part to undertake what suddenly appeared to be an act of madness. Yet through messages from the Tarot, most particularly the Hanging Man and Temperance, that view became transformed as I found myself absorbed.

As is usually the case, life has a habit of heading off in a different direction just at the point you think you should be doing something else, and settling down to write seemed to mark precisely such an occasion! The familiar world around me went into explosion mode, with a few spectacular gems thrown into the mix, just for good measure. At the time my own cards held the appearance of a disaster preview—and as ever, how accurate they were. Send in the cavalry! Enter loving family and friends, an encouraging and wonderful editor in the form of Barbara Moore, the team of helpful staff at Llewellyn led by an enthusiastic Bill Krause, and gradually the madness of the world slipped beyond the task at hand. Amidst the mayhem, as if by some unknown intervention, readers' letters continued to arrive, a timely reminder of the reasoning that led me here in the first place.

What became apparent from the many messages I received was the amount of readers who had been completely new to the world of Tarot, together with a number who had originally given up but returned. As an author, to touch so many lives in such a positive way, to act as a stepping-stone along the pathway that led people into this magical world that many of us already appreciate, was both a rewarding and humbling experience. I hope that within these pages you find the answers you were seeking and, as always, look forward to hearing of your progress.

Overview

How frequently the lines of theory and practice blur. Whether preparing a recipe or assembling flat pack furniture, have you ever noticed that sometimes things don't quite go the way the instructional manual said they would? You get there in the end, the desired result, but not quite in the way stated…or the way you intended when you first set out. (This sounds like a description of my map reading!) Then it shouldn't surprise you to know this can happen with Tarot too, as most experienced readers will tell you.

The readings that follow are presented to you as they happened at the time. As covered in *Easy Tarot,* all the readings open with the Anchor and Life Spread, which provides an overview of what is happening and potentially about to happen in the various areas of someone's life, with the Celtic Cross used for any further questions. This remains true to the format of the original book and so provides us with constancy as we see the various ways the spread applies to the different seekers' situations.

About This Book

This book is intended as a working and experiential guide taking the techniques used from *Easy Tarot* into real reading situations, so you can follow how they apply in practical application, just as if you were sitting right alongside me. The feedback and results show how those readings developed for the seekers, or not, as the case may be. Whilst the readings were recorded at the time with sound and images, my thoughts could not be, which resulted in hotfooting it to the computer as soon as they left, in order to capture and share the mental process that was experienced.

I was aware that due to the nature of this work there was the danger it could be misconstrued and so an important point I would like to highlight is that the aim of this book was *not* to prove that Tarot works—that was never the intention. Initially this aspect played heavily on my mind. In one sense, if the readings were left without the feedback it would be no different to the fictitious examples that are sometimes provided, but as most Tarot readers already know, often what we are confronted with in the cards may not compare to the easy flow provided in the manual. To a certain extent this may always be so, as it isn't possible to cover every combination of Tarot cards that may appear grouped together. Yet, by producing the results, it was almost as if I were setting the Tarot and myself to the test, putting us on the line and hanging us out to dry. As you can see, I had a few reservations.

Then just before I began, my cards went completely to pot—all three decks at the same time. Coincidence? Even my personal deck produced readings that made no sense, I had never experienced anything like this before; it was as if they wouldn't speak to me. I began to wonder if they were unimpressed by the plan that lay ahead. I had a Tarot revolution on my hands—the cards had gone on strike! I considered whether I was going to have to write to the publisher, although I was not quite sure how to rationally explain that one to my editor; odd, even by my standards.

I meditated upon them. I talked to them. (Confessional moment: I have always conversed with my cards.) I explained and even pleaded with them. I tried new decks, all seasoned, ready, and waiting to go. Same result. You have probably realised by now that it wasn't the cards. However much I thought I had rationalised them, my worries transferred to the decks because they were still sitting in my subconscious. I had a series of dreams ranging from my Tarot cards being ruined on windswept pavements, to poking out of a tiny grave in the rain, and each time a card was presented or featured quite strongly. Once I deciphered the dreams through reading the cards shown I realised what was happening, then all was well. Well, almost … the rest I shall reserve for Chapter 13.

What is presented to you here is my own method of reading, one that works well for me and those I have shared it with, but, as previously mentioned in the original book, I am not suggesting this is the only way to read Tarot cards. There are many different approaches taken by experienced readers, the Tarot is so diverse, as are the methods by those who read them. Within this lies the beauty of Tarot, the never-ending learning curve, the lively debate and exchange between Tarot lovers at every level, constantly learning from one another. The one area most readers usually fully agree upon is the ethics and principles surrounding the reading itself.

Editor's note: In order to give you, the reader, the experience of being with the author as she did this book's readings, all case studies appear mostly in the present tense. Hopefully you'll feel as though you are sitting right alongside Josie as she examines the cards, makes mental notes, and observes and converses with her clients.

In Search of
the Seekers

Eleven people feature in the case studies with their progress followed from the original reading to the conclusion of their results. They were selected due to their age, gender, and diverse backgrounds to provide as much variation as possible for you, and most had little experience or knowledge of Tarot previously.

A few have chosen to go public with their identity, whilst others appear anonymous due to the depth of personal information that was revealed and shared. Most found this aspect surprising, as you will see from some of their comments. In almost every case study there were further details, either in the reading or discovered from the results, that were too personal or involved third parties, and so were not published. For that reason, sometimes the difficulty lay in what we had to leave out, without affecting the authenticity or results of the reading.

In order to provide a glimpse of their own perspective they were also asked to share thoughts of their reading experience with you in their own words, once events had materialised. As readers we don't very often have access to the impact the reading has on the inquirer, their thoughts and feelings, outside of what they say at the time. I asked if they would convey this for you, concentrating upon the reading itself rather than my role within it.

Aside from the email reading, which was shown due to the unusual content, we started and finished with the original people, so they were not purposely chosen from a collection in order to supply the best results.

How to Get
the Best from This Book

Diagrams of all the spreads for each case study are provided and you may wish to lay out your cards as a copy of the spread that was in front of me as we work through each one. Personally, I feel you would find this helpful, as you will discover I move around the various cards in differing areas, so it will help you follow me as we work through the reading. Unlike a book format, where we cover one card or group of cards at a time, in real time reading situations there is a lot more movement. Trying to follow this in a listed format I am sure would be a little confusing and lose the true flow of the reading. Since with Tarot we work in the world of images I hope you will find the effect of the cards in front of you starting to make sense, realising the connections as we work through them.

The Card Meanings Used

By now you have probably developed your own meanings for the cards, so in your own reading situations the cards will respond to the interpretations you associate with them. At the back of the book you will find a brief summary of the card interpretations that I used in the readings for your reference. These are shortened versions from those supplied in the original *Easy Tarot* book. However, what you will find is that when using the cards for predictive readings it is easier if these are fairly concise, otherwise it can create too many variables.

A Quick Recap:
Some Important Bits and Bobs

Whilst this is in some way a continuation to the original book it was also intended that this study should stand on its own, for those who haven't read *Easy Tarot*. However, there are a number of areas that would be difficult to cover without some reference to the original material. So forgive me in advance, from both camps. I have attempted to strike a balance between providing bite-size chunks of relevant information, sufficient for what I have said or do here to make sense for you, but without duplicating pages of text from the original book. For those who followed the first book, the information should slot into place for you now as we move from theory into practice.

Your Own Tarot Book

Whether you chose to keep the Tarot diary was entirely your choice, as is everything I present or recommend to you. Just consider it like the shopping cart syndrome—when you browse a supermarket you only put the items you want into your shopping cart, you don't have to buy the whole store. So please take from this information what you feel is helpful to you.

I received many letters from people reporting that it was whilst keeping their Tarot diary that the pieces fell into place for them. So why did I recommend recording each individual card? Once we reach this level of reading it's quite important to thoroughly understand your cards and it would be a little difficult if you had to flick back and forth to check meanings in a book as you would lose the flow, particularly with the amount of cards present.

One of the techniques used is based upon a renowned learning principle, concerning how we retain information. There is a reference about this in a little bestseller called *Skill with People,* by Les Giblin. More recently this theory has been linked with "Whole Brain Learning," which you may have heard of. The basis of this theory is that it engages the different hemispheres of the brain, stimulating learning and the retention of information. By reading the information alone you retain only ten percent, but by being actively engaged in the process you retain ninety percent.

If you have not read *Easy Tarot,* here is a brief summary of the diary technique I recommended:

- Use a separate page to record each card and leave enough space so you can add more at a later date. A spiral bound book is the easiest to use because it stays flat whilst you're working.

- As you examine each individual card, hold it, or touch the picture with your fingers, whilst writing down the meaning as you say it out loud. You can use bullet points for the key meanings given in the book.

- Then personalise the cards based on your own experiences, to avoid simply memorising the cards. So if the recollection of a particular event that has happened to you is triggered by one of the card's meanings, make a note of it.

- You may find that experiences of people you know remind you of the card's meanings, so make a note of that too. This helps the cards feel more personal to you as they start to represent real situations instead of just words in a book.

- With the court cards, assign and list people you know to each card, based on the descriptions given.

People who had previously struggled with the courts found the last tip particularly hit home, as they could connect them to real people they could relate to.

For the dedicated who followed it, what you should have found is that within your Tarot diary you have, in effect, written your own Tarot book. This technique was based upon integrating the cards into your own life, so the Tarot became a living world of experiences that *you* could relate to, started by making bullet points with a few of my keywords but then developed into your own interpretation. No longer the basis of other people's meanings but now connected to your own experiences that would trigger immediate responses when you saw a card before you.

By also recording and dating your readings in your diary you created an entire learning journey, not only of things that happened to you but a reference to go back to, to enable you to connect the dots, of what you saw and what you missed. It is said that personal experience is the greatest teacher and, hopefully, this is what your Tarot diary delivered for you. It provides your own unique journey with a deck that speaks to you in a personal language, because it moves beyond words and into the emotive realms of recognition from your sensory memory bank.

When you add the final layer of recording any dreams or psychic development, which may have occurred naturally along the learning process, the Tarot diary proved valuable for those who took the time to follow it, despite the initial perception of a lengthy task. If you completed it, then my kudos to you!

Around the Tarot in Eighty Days

If the diary seems too daunting a task to add to your schedule, or it just doesn't suit your learning style, then the following technique might work for you. Consider it your own adventure as you embark upon a journey around the world of Tarot.

If you are still in the process of learning the card meanings, or feel you are struggling for time to do so, then it can be helpful not to feel overwhelmed to begin with. Breaking the task down into smaller steps can be more rewarding so you feel a sense of accomplishment. If you learnt only one card daily it would take you seventy-eight days to understand the meaning of your cards.

Working on that basis, try to limit yourself to only one card a day, so it stays clearly in your mind. Extract the card from the deck and see how many situations you observe, or what memories it may evoke, that apply to the meaning of the card taken from your chosen learning book. You could carry the card with you or place it in a visible place to act as a focal point and reminder. At the end of the day you may wish to reflect upon your findings. This is easier to do if you follow the organised numerical order of each suit, which is usually the way it is covered in most beginner books.

Once you have reached the final card spend the next couple of days going through your deck, firstly in the order you learnt them, then try the same thing with randomly chosen cards. Place your book aside and resist the initial urge to check yourself as you allow the image from the card to connect with you. Take your time but if you feel completely blank on any of the cards just place them to one side whilst you continue through the rest. Once you have completed the deck you can go back to any cards you put to one side and if you still can't connect with them then refer to your book for help. However, by the time you reach the last card you should feel a personal resonance and deeper understanding of your deck.

Taking this a step further, Janet Boyer introduces a method for beginners and experienced readers alike in *The Back in Time Tarot Book,* which invites you to take a past event from either your own life, the news, music or film, and re-enact the content with your Tarot cards. This playful yet deceptively thought-provoking technique allows you to become acquainted with the cards through association, offering a fun and fresh approach in becoming familiar with your chosen deck.

Yan Tan Tether[1]

Upon first making the transfer from ordinary playing cards to Tarot, I started with the Swiss IJJ Deck and *Tarot Cards for Fun and Fortune Telling,* by S. R. Kaplan, published by US Games Systems. That was over thirty years ago now and the only information available to me at the time. Many of the spreads used a dialogue, or non-positional approach, some with as many as fifty-six cards, so that was how I first learnt to read Tarot. The smallest set positional spread was seven cards and I found this more difficult than a dialogue spread of forty-two, which became my reading spread of choice in the early days. As I didn't know any differently I suppose I didn't have any mental barriers to overcome.

If you are used to smaller and fixed positional spreads, all I would recommend is to try and keep an open mind in trying a different approach. For the Life Spread you are reading sequences of cards, like sentences, so although the idea of twenty-one cards may sound

---

1 Yan Tan Tether is an ancient rhyming system and was traditionally used by Yorkshire shepherds for counting sheep. It originates from Brythonic Celtic language and means "one, two, three."

overwhelming, technically you are still reading them one at a time, just linked together, like phrases. But there is power in numbers, as I hope you will discover, from recurring themes that strengthen one another, to card associations as they sit side by side, content or unhappy with one another—like harmonious friends or grumpy bedfellows! I hope you will see the benefits for yourself as I take you through the readings, then as with everything, it is purely a matter of choice of what works and feels right for you.

Overview of the Spreads Used in the Readings

As we work through the readings I will be talking you through them, so far as possible showing where, how, and why I connected various cards or groups. What follows is an explanation of how to prepare these spreads and work through them, so you may feel a sense of repetition as we go through the case studies, as the intention was to take the theory and then show you how it works in practice. On the positive side, it means that you only have to get a brief grasp from the explanation of the spreads before seeing them in action!

About Reversed Cards

Using reversed cards is a matter of choice and since I prefer to read with upright cards this is how the readings here are presented. However, reversals add a further dimension to Tarot that you may wish to investigate before deciding whether to incorporate them into your own readings. *The Complete Book of Tarot Reversals,* by Mary Greer, provides a comprehensive and fascinating study into an area that can often be brushed aside too hastily. Together with Joan Bunning's *Learning Tarot Reversals,* these are presently the only two books dedicated solely to the upside down world of Tarot and offer enlightening perspectives you might wish to add to your Tarot library.

The Anchor

The Anchor acts as a point of reference throughout the readings and connects to the relevant named areas of the Life Spread. However, because the cards are all majors (taken from a separate deck) they can hold more influence. Named for its purpose throughout the readings, it remains in place even if the cards from the Life Spread are gathered up and then used for a spread to address a further question. It becomes a point of reference, and cross-reference, in relation to the Life Spread. Because it is made up of only the major arcana it can provide the final say in the matter, or act as a clarifying point to the details found in the Life Spread.

The Life Spread and The Anchor

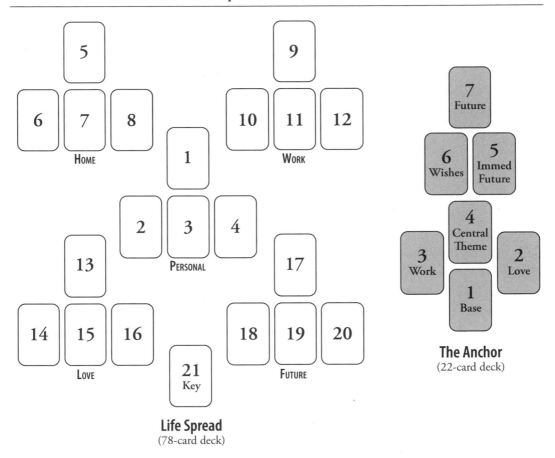

Life Spread
(78-card deck)

The Anchor
(22-card deck)

The first card in the Anchor is the base and foundation, and it makes the best place to start the whole reading. This is the seeker's current position based on what is happening around them and what they are currently experiencing.

On occasion you will find that the central theme, which acts like the heart of the reading, may still reflect the current conditions found in the first card—this in itself will tell you how much it is affecting the seeker. Preferably they should have moved on from the vibrations and atmosphere of the first card, so the central card will give an indication of what will become the central issue. However, as stated, some people get "stuck" in the present dilemma.

This can also hold true with the love and work areas. Someone experiencing an event that is traumatic or extremely important to them, in either area, may experience the atmosphere of this card for some time to come. In these instances the Immediate Future and Future cards are especially helpful to you in guiding the seeker.

Repeated cards found in both spreads can hold particular significance, in which instance you would focus on the theme and its relevance. However, should you find a repeat card in two *different* areas of both spreads it does not necessarily connect the two. For instance, the Hermit in the Love area of the Anchor and in the work area of the Life Spread. Sometimes there will be a connection but equally it can be a reoccurring theme that is, or will be, especially important to the seeker's life path.

The Life Spread

I devised the Life Spread many moons ago in an attempt to combat a number of restrictions found whilst reading. The Life Spread has no set positions as such, other than groups that are assigned with different areas of life. Each area has a Key card with a trio underneath which are then read as forward moving dialogue, always from left to right. The intention of the Life Spread and the Anchor was to enable more freedom from the cards to find expression, as against being squeezed into a positional meaning format, and equally, more freedom for the reader to move around the various areas as the interpretation and themes developed in the reading.

Areas of Life

The titles for each group cover the areas of life most people want to know about and provide the basis for a general reading without the need to ask questions of the cards at the outset, or worrying about phrasing questions correctly. Whilst each group of four cards holds a "title," i.e., personal, home, work, love, and future, another indicator found in this reading is when there are overriding themes. For someone about to be married, or divorced, you would tend to find that this spills over into most other areas. Equally, for someone wrapped up with work or financial worries. As a reflection of life, it is rarely lived neatly compartmentalised—that which affects us deeply tends to seep into every corner, sometimes flooding everything else.

For readings that appear chaotic or disjointed, jumping around all over the place, you will also find this usually mirrors events in the seeker's life. For some this is a temporary situation but I have known a few who have had regular consultations, where it is a constant and literally characterises their lifestyle or the way they deal with things—everything at once! With the groups of cards in front of you it is like looking into windows of the seeker's life and this overview alone can provide some extra insight. If you were using fixed positions representing past, present, future in each of the area groupings then these types of messages the cards can provide could be lost.

Starting Point

When you are first starting with this spread you may find it easier to read each area in rotation as it is laid out, beginning with the personal area then moving to home, then work, etc. As you feel more comfortable, and when there are some exciting influences evident together with the right feedback from the seeker, you will soon find yourself moving around the groups more easily.

I generally start with the personal area first, as I find it is rather like the base or foundation of the Anchor, it tends to reflect those issues that are uppermost in the person's mind. There is often a link between the base card of the Anchor and the personal area of the Life Spread, so it makes a good transition point to move over to the main spread after you have read the base card of the Anchor.

If you see a link from the personal area to one of the other groups in the Life Spread—for example, if it were love—you could move straight from there to the love and relationships area. It very much depends what you are faced with at the time.

You will note there is no particular "past—present—future," guideline provided for each of the grouped areas, as the timeline can vary slightly with each reading. However, the cards are always moving forward towards the future, from left to right in each group. I have found that the card to the far left of each group (positions 2, 6, 10, 14) often provides the immediate past or present influence still affecting the seeker, the following two cards continue reading into the future of how the situation is developing.

If you prefer a more definitive or positional approach then you may wish to designate the three cards in each area as past—present—future (except the final future cards: 17, 18, 19, 20.) Simply make this your set way of working with the Life Spread and the cards will oblige you. However, should you choose to take this approach, you can lose the flow of dialogue between the cards and the flexibility the reading can provide by limiting the amount of cards that can provide future information, and in fairness, that is usually what people want to know.

Role of the Key Cards

The card at the top of each group of three is known as the Key card. It is similar to the aforementioned card furthermost left, as it provides flavour and influence over the theme of that particular area. The seeker is usually already feeling the vibrations of this card, or if it is a court card, represents someone else involved in the situation. For this reason, you may occasionally find that the three cards below all relate to future influences.

From my descriptions you have probably noticed that these spreads rely upon feedback as you progress through the reading. Although I have done cold readings with these spreads, my preferred reading choice is interactive with the seeker, asking questions and inviting feedback as we go along, but only at the point I request it. Initially you are working blind, but I have found this helps to prevent preconceived ideas regarding their situation before starting. Sometimes what we know can make us question what we see in the cards, as the logic of the conscious mind can block the free flow associations coming from the subconscious.

Some Exceptions in the Life Spread

In some instances you will find that all the cards in the trio relate to a future incident, in which case the Key card should provide the flavour or connection. A further exception you may come across is when all the cards are informing you of one specific incident and they appear to "speak" as one. This may be unusual but tends to occur when there is an event of significance in the offing.

The Celtic Cross

This old favourite remains my spread of choice for any specific questions that may arise after the initial Life Spread reading because of the depth and timing it can reveal. I covered about sixteen pages on the Celtic Cross in *Easy Tarot,* which provides further techniques and insights as to how more information can be gleaned from the original ten positions and deciphering various sticking points people sometimes find with this spread. Given what I have already said, and to your doubtless vast relief, I won't be repeating them all here. I will explain how these apply as we go through the readings. (See p. 16 for the Celtic Cross layout.)

The Reader's Fan, shown as cards 11–14, may provide backup information to the main reading. These cards are not used as a continuation of the reading and sometimes they can seem to make little sense as they may relate to other situations surrounding the person being read for, but often they do reflect what is given in the main spread. If you do decide to use the Reader's Fan, regard it as an option that may provide more information for you. Sometimes it is quite stunning, in which case consider it a bonus—but don't get fixated on it if it isn't. I have only shown them here where there is an element of the reading present, so as not to confuse you, but I normally lay out the Reader's Fan in every Celtic Cross spread I do.

Timing System Used for the Celtic Cross

The Celtic Cross is the only spread I have found to work with the timing system I use, which is partially adopted from the full theory by Eileen Connolly in *Tarot: A New Handbook for the Apprentice,* who deserves full credit.

To provide a more specific timing you would need an ace to appear in positions five through nine in the Celtic Cross spread. The ace is read with the meaning first but then is also used as the timing card.

- Ace of Cups—from the beginning of March
- Ace of Wands—from the beginning of June
- Ace of Swords—from the beginning of September
- Ace of Pentacles—from the beginning of December
- For the amount of weeks use the number given in the tenth card, reduced to a single digit.
- If the tenth card is unnumbered (for instance a court card or the Fool) move backwards until you find the first numbered card.
- If you have more than one ace in the designated positions, always use the first ace.

Celtic Cross Diagram

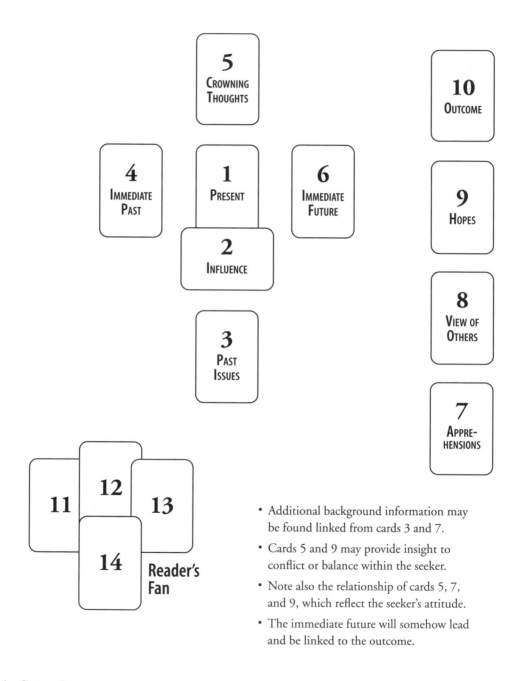

5 CROWNING THOUGHTS

10 OUTCOME

4 IMMEDIATE PAST

1 PRESENT

6 IMMEDIATE FUTURE

9 HOPES

2 INFLUENCE

8 VIEW OF OTHERS

3 PAST ISSUES

7 APPRE- HENSIONS

11

12

13

14 **Reader's Fan**

- Additional background information may be found linked from cards 3 and 7.
- Cards 5 and 9 may provide insight to conflict or balance within the seeker.
- Note also the relationship of cards 5, 7, and 9, which reflect the seeker's attitude.
- The immediate future will somehow lead and be linked to the outcome.

For example: Ace of Cups in the sixth position and the Hanging Man in position 10 would provide the timing of around three weeks from the beginning of March. If you are mathematically minded you have probably calculated that this limits a timeframe to thirty-six weeks of the year, since the largest single digit can be nine. However, we are providing an approximate timeframe, which allows some flexibility.

Using Two Decks for the Spreads

We will be using two decks simultaneously for the readings. One comprises of only the twenty-two majors removed from one deck and kept specifically for the Anchor. The second is a full seventy-eight card deck, which is used for the Life Spread.

More experienced readers may enjoy using two decks of different design for the Anchor and the Life Spread, but beginners might find it easier with two decks of the same type. For the purpose of the book, we are using two decks of the Gilded Tarot, as this is the format I use when reading for others. Firstly, because the Gilded is my working deck of choice, and secondly because people love the images and it is easier for them to see the likeness themselves when certain cards are repeated in the two spreads.

For personal use with self-readings I keep a completely separate set of decks, consisting of the Gilded as my main deck and the majors from Aleister Crowley's Thoth deck for the Anchor Spread. So feel free to use whatever feels comfortable for you and is your preference.

Preparation for the Life Spread and the Anchor

- The deck consisting of twenty-two major cards are shuffled first without asking any questions.

- Prepare the deck in your usual way. My preference is to let the seeker shuffle the cards and then ask them to cut the deck into three, from left to right, allowing the cards to drop through their fingers, holding them just above the table.

- Gather the cards back up—the first pile dropped is collected first, with the second placed underneath and then the third under this. Set this stack face down to the right of the table.

- Repeat the process with the second deck of seventy-eight cards.

- Once completed place the second deck to the left of the table.

- The Anchor is not laid out until the full process of shuffling and cutting has been completed with both decks, to avoid the seeker being distracted by the card images.
- Take the first deck of majors and lay them out into the Anchor, as shown, then place the remainder of the deck out of the way.
- The Anchor will stay in place throughout the entirety of the readings.
- Take the full second deck and lay out as shown for the Life Spread. Place the remainder of the pile face down to your left of the table, as this deck will be used again if further questions are required.

Breaking It Down

If the Life Spread and Anchor are a long way from your usual style of reading, one of the ways you can become more accustomed to the dialogue approach is to practice by using only four cards to begin with, reading for yourself. Once you feel more comfortable with the process, transfer to the full twenty-one cards that make up the Life Spread.

When you have progressed to the full Life Spread you can then add the Anchor alongside. Personally, I would feel lost without the Anchor, but my daughter, Emily, presently reads without it and is still happy with the results she achieves for people.

As with most things there comes the moment when you need to allow a sense of adventure and follow our friend the Fool, take a leap of faith and jump right in. It may feel a little strange to begin with but that's natural if it falls outside of your familiarity and comfort zone. Like most, I am sure you have some willing close friends who would be happy for you to take them on a test drive, once you have found your bearings from some self-readings.

Additional Considerations

Who Shuffles the Cards?

Some readers like the seeker to shuffle the cards, yet others prefer that no one else touches their deck, and some readers cut the deck whilst others do not. There is no right or wrong way, just your preference, so you may like to experiment with different methods until you find what feels right and works best for you. In face-to-face readings I prefer the seeker to shuffle the cards.

If you are undecided, here are a few options you could consider trying:

- The seeker shuffles and cuts the cards.
- The seeker mixes up the cards face down on the table before selecting the amount of cards you require.
- You shuffle the cards and decide when to stop.
- You shuffle the cards and the seeker tells you when to stop.
- You shuffle the cards and lay them in a line or fan, face down, and let the seeker choose the required number of cards needed for the spreads.

The Opening Process

Most people will probably have developed their own silent opening statement before starting a reading. In *Easy Tarot* I covered opening for guidance and using a crystal but will cover my own process for you here briefly.

I prefer the backdrop of a plain dark reading cloth to lay the cards upon and place a small clear quartz crystal at the top. The crystal has already been programmed and blessed to keep the working space free from negative energy and to help receive clear guidance to assist those who come to consult the Tarot.

Once I have explained what is going to happen (covered in detail for you on page 23), I cut the deck into three piles, restack, and begin to shuffle. Whilst shuffling the cards I say the following in my mind, "I call upon the Higher Realms of Light, as a child of Light, to bring me guidance, protection, and assistance. Please help me to receive clear guidance in this reading to assist (seeker's name.) Thank you." Then I cut the deck into three again, demonstrating to the seeker how I would like them to do it once they feel ready, and then hand them the deck to start shuffling. The silent opening statement helps me stay focussed whilst creating a connection with the seeker on a spiritual level.

If you feel yourself becoming flustered or if you realise your focus has become more about you and your reading, rather than the seeker, then repeating your opening statement quietly in your mind can help calm you down, bring you back into the moment and your purpose in the reading. Calling upon something we consider a higher power than ourselves can be soothing and helps to put things back in perspective. For you this may be the universe, the source, the light, an angel, God, the Goddess, whatever is comfortable for you and your beliefs.

Another tip I have found useful is that if I find myself struggling with a card I will be honest and tell the seeker I don't know how it fits into their reading. You will see me do this in some of the case studies. So you see, don't feel as if you need to have all the answers—what is obscure to you may make perfect sense to them.

A Little Help from Your Friends: Get Support

If you are just getting started you probably think that experienced readers always know exactly what is front of them, that everything goes well every time, that they never go blank, or that they never have "Aha!" moments *after* the reading! Most will tell you that sometimes it happens to them too. Some of us may even have a past experience we would rate as a cringe factor ten! So please do not think that these types of experiences are only reserved for beginners. As you will see, I will be sharing some of my "moments" with you here as they occurred in the readings.

There are many wonderful resources available now for all levels of Tarot readers where you can learn, discover and explore new techniques, investigate different decks, share experiences and get support. With recognised associations, groups, workshops, websites and online forums, there is something for everyone, on and offline, with plenty of kind and thoughtful souls in the Tarot community who are happy to lend support or point you in the right direction. With Tarot we all feel that we are constantly learning from one another along the way, so wherever you go you should find yourself amongst friends.

If you don't have access to a group or if this is not your preference, then you could always enlist the support of a Tarot buddy. For many years a friend and I have met regularly for a scheduled evening when we do readings for one another and discuss the many aspects of Tarot. Learning and sharing your findings with others of like mind can be fun and supportive. So don't feel you need to go it alone, there is plenty of help and support available in the Tarot community.

There is always the risk that by quoting a few I miss out many others, but it would be impossible to list so many good resources here. However, if you pay a visit to the following main associations you will find recommendations for many more sources you can explore. As non-profit organisations they are inexpensive to join and seek to inform, educate, and promote Tarot in a positive, ethical way.

- TABI—The Tarot Association of the British Isles—www.tabi.org.uk
- ATA—The American Tarot Association—www.ata-tarot.com

Ethics and Responsibility

If you are a member of either of the above Tarot associations, you will already be familiar with their code of ethics; if you are not yet a member both ATA and TABI provide a copy of readers' ethics displayed on their respective websites. ATA also helpfully provide an excellent "Ethical Tarot Statement" which is available for download and printing, it contains educational information for the public concerning Tarot and also a Code of Ethics for readers.

Regardless of whether you decide to join these associations, please take the time to read the ethics they promote because they cover so many areas that should be considered when reading for others. Following a code of ethics is important to everyone in the Tarot community to ensure the positive promotion of Tarot with responsible and professional practice. As it is also designed to protect both you and your seeker, you may wish to display a code of ethics or incorporate it into an introductory flyer, alongside what people may expect from the reading and how you work.

As you progress you may find it helpful to have national helpline telephone numbers of registered organisations that you can refer to people if required, where they can get professional advice that falls outside of your qualifications or responsibility as a reader, such as: financial and debt counselling, domestic violence, addictions, health service, police, legal or criminal investigation department. In England we are fortunate to have access to free national organisations such as the Citizen's Advice Bureau, which covers a whole host of eventualities, and also the Samaritans for those who may feel they are having difficulty coping with life. If you personally recommend an individual, such as a chartered accountant or counsellor, it would be wise to only do so if you can personally vouch for their services, for obvious reasons.

In our role as readers we are trying to be helpful to those who consult us by opening their awareness to the potential and possibilities in the situations that may surround them. In empowering them we are not taking over the responsibility to make their own choices or decisions by telling them what to do, but we can advise areas where we feel care or further investigation would be advantageous. I may appear to state the obvious here, but most the time it is just a case of using common sense and considering the consequences of how the seeker may apply what you tell them.

As a general rule, you should not provide specific medical, legal, or financial advice—even if you are a qualified professional in one of those areas. It is best to have a clear distinction between your role as a reader and any other professional capacity during a reading. Doing otherwise can seem tempting at times, especially when people may have a legal or financial situation around them or showing in their reading. But, for instance, there is quite a difference between making the suggestion of showing caution with finances versus advising someone to sell all their shares. If you start providing specific advice that should be supplied by a professional, you could incorrectly advise someone with unfortunate results, or find yourself in a difficult situation. Some of these issues made appearances in the case studies; hopefully they'll provide some insight as to how they were dealt with.

Personally, I never provide a reading to a question concerning health matters. Should someone ask for a reading regarding their health, I will ask if they have a medical condition or reason to be concerned and suggest they make an appointment with their own doctor or ring a health service helpline, if appropriate.

The other area I do not cover is a request to read the cards for someone who is not present and did not request the reading, such as a divorcée who wanted to know if her ex-husband's girlfriend was having an affair. Ideally, any question can include someone who is directly involved in the seeker's life; after that it is how the question is phrased, but consider the possibility of prying. If a person is involved in the seeker's situation and the court card presents itself in the Celtic Cross (particularly the tenth position, which shows that the answer relies upon that person's actions), I may do a continuation reading from that card, but the reading still remains for the seeker. Otherwise I feel it is like an invasion of privacy and is an example of one of my own boundaries I am not comfortable to cross.

Something I have found helpful is that many years ago I took a counselling course and certification, mainly due to the situations I found myself confronted with whilst involved doing spiritual healing. The skills learnt proved valuable in reading situations, such as: how to really listen to someone, how to not tell people what to do, how to remain in an empathic position of non-judgement, and the importance of professional detachment. I am not suggesting it is something you *need* to do, but if you ever have the opportunity to attend a basic counselling course, I highly recommend it.

Between Readings

To ensure that the cards were "cleansed" between different people's readings, I separated them thoroughly beforehand, to ensure we received no mixed results. Normally I will use a number of decks and shuffle and cut them a few times before using them with a new seeker. However, I used a more methodical approach with these readings that I felt worked very well and you might wish to adopt.

Take the deck and deal the cards individually from the top into five positions. Work from left to right, one to five and then repeat:

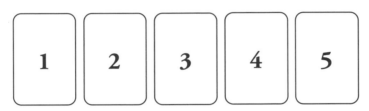

Once all the cards have been dealt and you are left with five stacks, pick them up in the following order, placing one stack underneath the other: 4, 2, 5, 3, 1. Then shuffle well and cut into three.

Your deck is now thoroughly cleansed and ready for you to start with a new person, without the concern that some of the cards may still be left in order from the previous seeker's reading. You would then start with the opening process (as previously described.)

What I Covered with the Seekers

As we will be following the readings as they happened I thought it would be best to cover what I go through with everyone before a reading, to avoid repetition with each case study. What you will find is that I do repeat some of these points throughout their readings (mainly concerning personal choice and the future) and have left those in, as they are a true account and I hope provide an essence of how they apply.

Before starting the opening process or the reading I ask seekers whether they have had a Tarot reading before, when it was, and how they found their experience. This helps uncover any preconceptions they may have about Tarot. I cover what is going to happen in the session and the way I work in order to make them feel comfortable by knowing what to expect. I explain that it is an interactive process and will require some feedback as we progress, to try to ensure the best results for them in how the messages given by the cards may apply to their situation. In order to do this I will be asking them questions or may ask them to expand upon a situation as it arises. The content of their reading or any information they share with me is confidential. I let them know they can stop me at any time if they have a question or do not understand something.

Then I go on to explain that the Tarot can provide the potentiality of a situation, which is similar to the domino effect, where past and present actions are developing into the future. This means that the future holds possibilities that can be shaped by their own actions. So for instance, if it appears to be heading in a direction they want to avoid they can consider their options and make changes that could ultimately shape where things are heading. I always say that "the Tarot are a wonderful guide but they are not your master. Only you can decide what is right for you. No one else has responsibility for your actions or choices."

Finally, I explain that the Tarot normally show the areas that are most relevant at the time and usually cover up to a six month period although some situations can take up to a year to unfold. Once we have completed the reading and if they have any further questions we can look at anything they may consider important or wish to explore further. My intention is to provide them with what I hope they will find to be an uplifting reading, offering the opportunity to explore choices in their life experiences.

With everything covered, I always ask if they feel happy to proceed and wait for their agreement before doing so. Then I start the opening process and show them how to handle the cards.

For the purpose of the book and to provide you with an introduction to the seeker, I asked their age, if they were in a relationship and currently working before starting, but do not always do this in private appointments. I usually ask somewhere in the reading, depending on the cards in front of me.

And So to the Seekers

So, with all the formalities and preliminaries now covered, I hope you will find the following readings and explanations helpful as you follow them through to their conclusion.

The Gay Man

imon is a single gay man, in his late thirties and the owner of a number of hair salons based in the south of England. He has had a Tarot reading previously so was quite open-minded and excited about having a reading.

First Impressions

As I put the cards down and took a moment to assess what was in front of me, these were the immediate thoughts that registered before I started relaying the cards to Simon:

- The Lovers at the base of the Anchor, repeated in the Life Spread in the future section.

- Personal, relationship, and future areas of Life Spread all focus on relationships.

- The Temperance card and Judgement in the Anchor's love area and central to the reading suggest the possibility of a reconciliation or revival. Also the Knight of Pentacles at the end of the Life reading, connected to relationships.

- The Fool repeated in the future area of both spreads.

- Work area of the Life Spread indicated concern, as it looked quite turbulent.

- Three tens—a period of transition to completion.

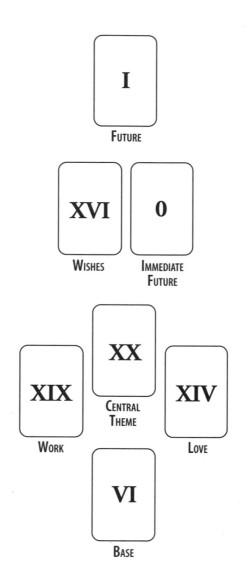

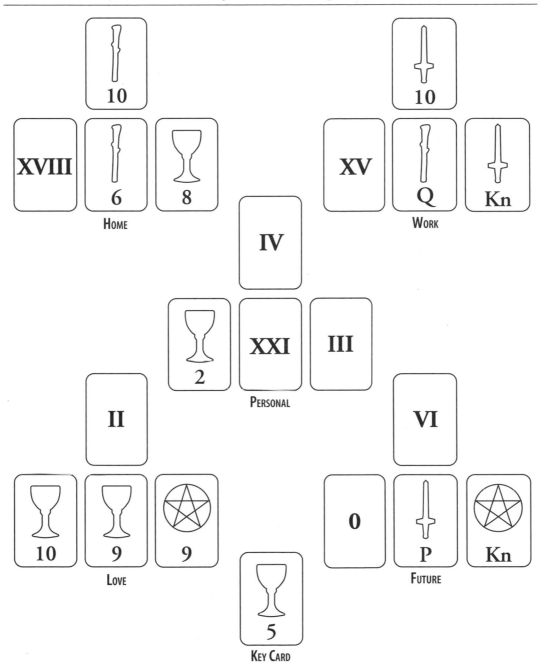

The Anchor
Base Position: The Lovers

The first card in the base position of the Anchor usually provides an indication of what is happening around the seeker, or of most importance to them at the time of the reading, and for this reason it is where I begin. I pointed out to Simon the Lovers in the foundation position and mention that relationships were repeated and strongly indicated in other areas of the Life Spread, which appeared to show that a relationship situation could be dominating his life at the moment. Simon agreed this was the case.

Once I had his confirmation it made it easier for me to proceed with more confidence that we were on the right track and, since so many areas referred to it, this was the trail I followed. The advantage of these two readings together is that you can move around the spreads in any order that you choose, often dictated by the cards or situations that appear. It isn't very often that I need to go through the spreads in a systematic way, area by area, as most people consult the cards for a reason and it usually reveals itself.

The Anchor
Love Area: Temperance
Central: Judgement

Temperance in the love area of the Anchor indicates a harmonious relationship but perhaps also the need for patience. As the card for balanced emotions and healing it can often bring about reconciliation in a relationship. With Judgement as the heart of the Anchor spread this strengthened the possibility that this was in some way a love revived, or that it held roots in the past.

Moving across to the Life Spread, you will notice the Two of Cups in the personal area. As this is a two and with the absence of the Ace of Cups (which would show the start of the relationship) it usually represents a close relationship that has already begun, or a continuation in some way. There are further indications here, but if we look at the personal area in total it may perhaps show the flow beginning to unfold:

The Life Spread
Personal Area: The Emperor,
Two of Cups, The World, The Empress

As the first card of the reading, the Emperor is the Key card, or consolidation card, for the personal area. Whether or not Simon realises it, this appears to place him in quite a powerful position in his situation. As a card of leadership and authority it also shows logical and rational thinking with regard to a situation, or that this is being called for.

The Two of Cups shows growth in a relationship. Following the message of Temperance, it also echoes harmony, balance, and kindness—a lovely bond between two people. It usually symbolises progression in a relationship and can sometimes represent a friendship, or other close bond, developing into something deeper.

Simon confirmed that this relationship was a developing situation and had been ongoing for more than a year. The closeness that was shared included daily contact but had not yet developed into a full relationship.

The World and the Empress blend well together here, with the message of success and triumph. The World usually suggests that this is not overnight success, but something that has been worked toward over a period of time, finally reaching conclusion. The Empress also shows bringing things to fruition but it is through a nurturing attitude, requiring a good deal of care and attention. With three major cards in one area this is quite powerful. A further link here, between the Empress in the Life Spread and Temperance in the Anchor, appeared to strengthen the message that patience, gentleness, and nurturing would be required in order to bring about the desired success.

The Life Spread
LOVE AREA: THE HIGH PRIESTESS, TEN OF CUPS, NINE OF CUPS, NINE OF PENTACLES
The Anchor
LOVE AREA: TEMPERANCE

Going back to my immediate impressions of the cards, at first glance the High Priestess was probably a key indicator I missed at that stage. Here she sits as our Key card in the love area. The High Priestess represents hidden knowledge, potential as yet unfulfilled and often, an aspect of secrecy. In readings it can represent a situation or information being revealed to the seeker that will be to their benefit once known, a secret being revealed to them.

At this stage, Simon volunteered the information that the relationship was not out in the open and this was an important aspect of everything. There were no cards to suggest an affair here, or other people involved in the relationship, so this didn't appear to be a reason for the secrecy that surrounded it. With otherwise beautiful cards, the Ten and Nine of Cups suggested that this relationship held a great deal of promise for emotional happiness and certainly what Simon was most hoping for, indicated by his wish card, the Nine of Cups.

There is usually a point in the reading where the seeker naturally feels drawn into revealing more about themselves and their situation; up until this stage I will usually only ask for basic confirmation. This is to ensure I'm heading in the right direction but also because if they reveal the entire situation to me too soon then quite often information that the cards provide has already been given to me by them—and this could cause them to question what they are being told. ("Well, I just told her that!") By not knowing the full circumstances of their situation it prevents perception from being coloured, as the logical mind can then cause us to question what we may see as improbable, based on what we know.

The relevance of many aspects of the reading so far came together here. Simon and his potential partner shared a very deep friendship and involvement in each other's lives, but his partner held fears of coming out about his sexuality, mainly because of the effect he felt it would have on his family. For this reason, the relationship hadn't fully developed. Simon had struggled with this initially and earlier had tried to dismiss the relationship as frustratingly going nowhere, but had felt no inclination to pursue other relationships.

Temperance now makes a great deal more sense in the love area, through Simon's patient, understanding, and loving nature toward his partner, as he waited for him to make the next step. Judgement as the revival card rang true, since his partner had recently called him in the early hours expressing a need to talk, even though he couldn't fully do so at the time. Since they are in contact every day, Simon knew the reason for the call was to raise the unfulfilled aspect of their relationship and that this issue was about to be resurrected. He wasn't sure how the situation would develop and at times questioned his own peace of mind.

From what we have found in the cards so far the future indications are good. Moving back to the love area, the Nine of Pentacles may suggest there is yet a period of time when Simon will appear to operate independently. Whilst this Nine indicates someone who is materially and emotionally secure within themselves, in their own right and through their own efforts, it does not necessarily show that they are alone or without relationships. However, I felt it showed that in certain respects Simon would still be seen as an independent person—so the status quo might remain for a while longer. For instance, this may have been different if we had the Ten of Pentacles instead of the Nine, or if the Ten of Cups had followed the Nine of Cups instead of the Nine of Pentacles.

The Life Spread
FUTURE AREA: THE LOVERS, THE FOOL, PAGE OF SWORDS, KNIGHT OF PENTACLES
The Anchor
IMMEDIATE FUTURE: THE FOOL

Since the final part of the Life Spread also focussed upon the relationship it felt the natural path for the reading to take and was therefore the area that I covered next.

With the Lovers as the Key card it informs us that the main focus is about the relationship. The Fool is represented in both spreads, as it sits in the immediate future position of the Anchor too. This shows us that an unexpected opportunity will present itself soon that will demand Simon make a choice—whether or not to follow the situation the Fool brings. People often feel they are ready for the Fool card in their life, yet when the situation presents itself, they can naturally hold back, as it is unknown territory or a situation jumps into play at a time they were least expecting. We are generally creatures of habit who like things to follow a natural sense of order, but what the Fool brings (or when) can quite often feel as if it is out of the blue, or not in the way the seeker anticipated.

The Page of Swords appears at odds with the Fool, since it can represent delays or disappointing news and the Fool is often a positive card. The Knight of Pentacles shows something finally coming to fruition that may have dragged on for a long time, to the point that the person may have virtually given up. It usually represents a situation where the seeker has invested a good deal of time and energy, methodically and carefully. This would certainly seem to apply to Simon's position. So overall, the situation may soon move towards a conclusion, perhaps in circumstances that seem unexpected and possibly not in a way he would have considered perfect. I felt the important part here was not to be put off by whatever the Page of Swords would bring, as there were so many other positive aspects in the rest of the spreads. It would seem that the unexpected situation brought in by the Fool has an element of disappointing news (Page of Swords), but it is through this that the conclusion from the Knight of Pentacles is found. Transition towards completion is also a theme found from the three tens in the spread.

The Life Spread
WORK AREA: TEN OF SWORDS, THE DEVIL, QUEEN OF WANDS, KNIGHT OF SWORDS
The Anchor
WORK AREA: THE SUN

Since this was such a strong area of the spread, I felt drawn to cover this part of the reading next. It was also quite significant that the Sun, a success card, appeared in the Anchor, which seemed completely at odds with the cards in the Life Spread. It looked as though whatever situation was brewing in the work area thankfully did not appear to upset the whole scheme of things in the longer term, because the Sun is such a strong card. Due to the Anchor being made up of only the majors it is always the place of reference and confirmation.

The Ten of Swords as our Key card suggests quite a significant disappointment, or at worst, the ending of a situation and perhaps ruined plans. The Devil placed before the Queen of Wands indicates the person that the problem lies with, and the general feeling surrounding this person is clearly not good; there can also be an aspect of secrecy with this card, perhaps indicating that she has secret plans. With the Knight of Swords the suggestion is that once the situation occurred it would unravel fairly rapidly, perhaps creating a certain amount of chaos. This is where the situation shows it is leading to but before revealing this to Simon I need to know his current position.

I ask Simon if there has been an ending or significant disappointment recently connected to his work. Simon tells me he cannot place this so I move on to the Devil, since it would appear the Ten of Swords is still to follow, unless he has not yet recognised a situation and this can sometimes happen in retrospect. I explain that this may be connected to a lady, whom I would describe to him, but also tell him there may have been some bad feeling or an aspect of secrecy surrounding her. I use the personality type first and then ask Simon if he recognises the person from this description. The Queen of Wands is a warm, cheerful individual who is always busy with a number of projects at once. She appears to thrive upon this schedule, but it can make her appear somewhat disorganised at times.

Simon now recognises the situation and the lady concerned as a new employee in a senior position in one of his salons. He had noticed a few things appeared amiss recently, financial and otherwise, that fell outside the usual patterns of the business that coincidentally started at the same time she began. He had employed her because he felt she would bring a new and innovative side to his business, which he had invested in considerably and had high hopes for, with the intention of exploring further. He felt this was now doubtful and had some serious concerns.

The circumstances do seem to connect to the cards we are being shown, so now I feel more comfortable to reveal the situation as I see it before me. With the Ten of Swords I tell Simon that I feel this association will come to an end and the Knight of Swords suggested that this could come about sooner than he was expecting, or that when the ending came there would be a certain swiftness surrounding it, as this Knight often brings a degree of speed and chaos into the equation. Since he has not yet experienced the Ten of Swords then it certainly seemed to show that an ending would result. The Devil surrounding the Queen of Wands may show his suspicions concerning her and his reasons for them, but it could still represent that she has secret plans. However, the Sun in the Anchor indicates that overall his business should not suffer and would continue to be successful.

Simon confirmed that his salons were doing well and, whilst a disappointment, he hoped the loss should not affect his business as a whole. Her departure would create some problems as he had invested considerably into developing the new side of the business. However, given his recent misgivings, he felt that there was every possibility that the association could come to an end.

The Life Spread
HOME AREA: TEN OF WANDS, THE MOON, SIX OF WANDS, EIGHT OF CUPS

In the home area, the Ten of Wands as the Key card shows there is something Simon is finding overwhelming or overburdening. The Moon suggests fluctuating emotions and perhaps some uncertainty. Simon could not connect to this in his home life and so I continued. I explained that it would seem that the feelings of burden and fluctuating emotions could be connected to a situation that may have brought some good news, that initially he felt happy about and brought a sense of personal achievement.

Once I had added the interpretation from the Six of Wands, Simon informed me he had recently purchased another property and felt very pleased with himself over the price he had paid. At the time he thought he would move into it as his home, but having gone through the process was now uncertain. He hadn't made the connection because it is not where he lives and hadn't made the association with his home life. Ideally, he would like his partner to move in with him but otherwise his earlier excitement had diminished. He said that whilst the property sat empty it weighed on his mind, a reminder of what he really wanted and hoped for: the home he would share with his partner. He agreed that the meanings of the Ten and the Moon accurately reflected his thoughts and feelings about the house.

The Eight of Cups indicates walking away from a situation due to disillusionment or disappointment, and usually represents a form of abandonment in favour of a different path. The Six of Wands is surrounded by less positive cards here, so the good feeling is limited by the other emotions being felt. With the Eight of Cups as the final card of this area the present indications are that he would move away from this property in the future. Whether this would be from renting it out or selling it I could not say, but currently the suggestion is that he would not be making this his home.

Simon says that in the back of his mind he had realised the house purchase had been an emotional decision and probably not very logically placed. Although he knows he would not make a loss on the property financially it was emotionally disappointing, due to his real reasons for buying it. He explains that he had completely refitted and furnished the house, but felt sad when he went there; he couldn't bring himself to move in on his own. I quietly listen to his sadness as he chastises himself for what he thinks sound like unrealistic and stupid dreams. I tell him we are all prone to feel like fools in the eyes of love but, if it were any consolation, I would be completely bowled over if someone had gone to that much trouble because of how they felt about me. This lightens the mood and he says if he were straight, he would marry me in a shot. We both start laughing.

The Life Spread
KEY CARD: FIVE OF CUPS
The Anchor
HOPES AND WISHES: THE TOWER

I found the Key card a little curious; the reading looked quite positive. Although Simon may not quite get the result he was hoping for with his relationship, it didn't seem to relate to a Five of Cups moment. The Key card does not always relate to a future event and can represent how the seeker is feeling about a situation or his general attitude. This is clearly important, as it can show what is affecting them or preventing them from achieving what they most desire.

The Five of Cups can indicate feelings of disappointment or loss. The figure in the card is focussed upon the three spilled cups, representing that which he feels has been lost, rather than the positive factors still at work shown in the two upright cups behind him. There is a danger here in becoming buried in past aspects of a situation and missing the good that still remains. Simon confirmed that the earlier fears he encountered with his partner still worried him, in case the situation merely repeated itself.

The Tower in the wishes area of the Anchor is also a strong indicator. It can sometimes appear confusing when someone draws what is perceived to be a negative card in the wish position. How can that be? I have found that the Tower or Death in this placement shows when people desire radical change in an ongoing situation that is weighing them down (for instance, a person going through a divorce or messy break-up quite often has one of these cards in this position). Because they are such powerful cards, and the type most of us wish to avoid, it tends to give an idea of the level of anxiety some people may be inwardly experiencing. So together, the Five of Cups and the Tower provide us with further insight as to how Simon is really feeling about the relationship situation and how important this is to him.

The Anchor
FUTURE: THE MAGICIAN

The Magician in the final outcome position of the Anchor provides Simon with the message of having confidence in his own ability to handle situations; he already has all the talents and ability that he needs within himself, he just needs to have confidence within that. Whilst a good card for his business concerns it can relate to any area of life. In saying this, I take him back to Temperance and the Empress from the Anchor in the love area and his personal section of the Life Spread. He has already handled the situation well so far and would indicate more of the same for a while in order to achieve his goal—patience and nurturing. Simon felt this provided a great deal of reassurance to his situation and stated that having waited this long he thought he could wait a bit longer.

Summary

Having concluded everything I could see in the two spreads, and before gathering up the cards, I asked Simon if there was anything further he wished to clarify with me from the reading, or anything else he wished to know by asking a question of the cards. Simon felt clear on everything we had covered but wanted to know if we may be able to get a little bit more about the relationship from another reading and perhaps a clearer sense of timing. With the Life Spread, I have found that the results usually follow within a three to six month timescale, although some events can be as much as twelve months. However, the Celtic Cross can provide a more definite time indication, if the relevant cards we need show.

Additional Spread: Celtic Cross

Rather than specifically ask the cards to provide timing I suggested that Simon ask his question as to what was the future of the relationship. This way it was possible that we may receive a timing card within the spread anyway, but failing this we could take the reading on one stage further to specifically ask. Although I advised Simon that if no timing cards appeared by that point, then it was unlikely that we would receive one.

Since his question specifically concerned his relationship with someone else, I covered the four different personality types of the kings. This way we could identify his partner beforehand, so there would be no indecision if any of the male court cards were presented in the reading. It was decided that Simon is the King of Wands and his partner the King of Pentacles.

Simon shuffled the cards whilst asking what the future of the relationship with his partner was. Here were the cards for the response to the question. It is interesting how much of this reading confirms what we have now been told; often you will find this to be true.

The Five of Cups in the starting position shows what Simon is experiencing in relation to the question, his fears concerning the past of this relationship. However, the card that crosses it acts like a filter. In this instance we have Justice, which shows the need for a balanced and logical mind.

The basis for the situation (card 3) often ties in with the card in the seeker's apprehensions, (card 7) supplying a snapshot of a past situation that is influencing the present position. The Fool together with the Page of Wands reveals the unexpected message, the phone call that has triggered the current situation and Simon's emotions shown in the first and second cards.

The most recent past, or the influence just passing through, (card 4) that Simon is currently experiencing is the Moon. This shows us his fluctuating emotions and some confusion within himself. It also holds the message that there is a lot more depth to a situation than can presently be seen.

A further connection can often be found in the crowning thoughts (card 5) and card 9 of hopes. The Eight of Cups and the Knight of Wands show Simon's consideration in abandoning his plans to move into the property he has bought, as the Knight of Wands often represents a change of residence. However, when also taken in the context of its own position and connection to the question, the seeker's thoughts can often lead to a potential course of action

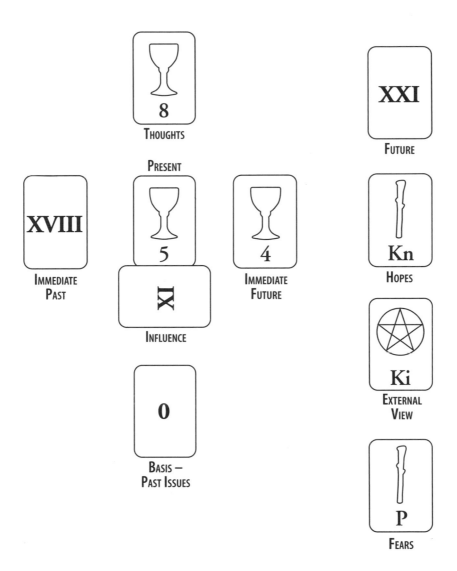

manifesting, in this instance the cards indicate Simon strongly considering abandoning the effort he has put into the relationship so far.

Taking it one stage further, the seeker's attitude can be seen by taking the crowning thoughts (card 5), apprehensions (card 7), and their hopes (card 9.) In this reading we have three cards from the minor arcana in those positions. We can also see some conflict in Simon's feelings: the thoughts of abandoning the situation and walking away, whilst the Page of Wands is a positive card in a "negative" position showing his desire to hear good news yet also fearing he may not, with the Knight of Wands following the Page, bringing action to the news and his hoped for change of home.

In the immediate future, the Four of Cups warns Simon to be careful not to miss an opportunity due to the way he may be feeling. The sixth card, as the immediate future, is often already in the process of "lining up" since this event has already been influenced by the most recent past and present, actions already taken or reactions to things that have already happened, so the results of the sixth card can sometimes be difficult for the seeker to change as it is already in the process of materialising.

Looking at the sequence of the Five of Cups (present influence), the Moon (recent past), and the Eight of Cups (crowning thoughts), the feeling of discontent often experienced by the Four of Cups appears to show a natural progression that makes sense.

One of the most interesting cards was the King of Pentacles situated in the eighth position, as we had previously established this as the court card that represented his partner. Simon's partner is an accountant and his personality type also closely matches the one I use for the King of Pentacles. In the eighth position we can see that his partner feels strongly about the situation.

In the final position of card ten we have the World. This brings the reassuring message of a successful outcome and final conclusion. As both cards six and ten represent a future situation they are usually strongly linked in the chain of events, so it is especially important that Simon heeds the message from the Four of Cups, as his natural inclination may draw him to give up (Eight of Cups in the fifth and Four of Cups in the sixth position).

Whilst the World may be a major card and usually holds the more powerful energy we cannot dismiss the influence found in the messages from the cards showing the seeker's attitude and feelings; even though they are minor cards the messages found here can dampen or drag down the World's usual interpretation. In addition, the Five of Cups in the present, and the Moon most recently passing through, add to Simon's apprehensions over the situation. Once more I feel this represents considerable effort from Simon to attain. The Four of Cups informs us of this too, but the message appears to be echoed from the additional areas when looked at more closely.

Using the Anchor for further clarification we have Temperance in the love area, Judgement as the central issue, and the Fool in the immediate future, so it does appear an opportunity will present itself and these cards strengthen the World found at the end of the Celtic Cross. Taking all these factors into consideration produces quite a mixed message, so the potentiality certainly appears to exist but Simon's apprehensions could cast doubt on the outcome. In order to achieve his aim he would need to be more positive about the situation and, as the Empress informed us from the Life Spread, the way in which the results of the World is attained appears to be from Simon's nurturing of the relationship.

TAKING IT ONE STAGE FURTHER

Since we had no timing card, I took the World and placed it in the first position so we could continue the reading. The rest of the cards were gathered up and the deck given back to Simon to shuffle. This time he asked the cards for a continuation reading with a timing—and when the cards were placed I could see we had received one!

This was a very positive continuation reading. In this situation we are moving further forward in time as we have taken the last card, which represented the future outcome. So all the positions need to be read in relation to that fact. Therefore, the first card represents the present situation that will cover the World. In effect, the reading is based on what will happen *if* the World manifests, it is like opening a door to see what would happen next.

The Ace of Wands in the covering position indicates a whole new beginning, with plenty of excitement and enthusiasm. Furthermore, the crossing card or filter, is the Nine of Cups, otherwise known as the "wish card."

As the basis of what will be the past situation the Six of Wands is the bearer of good news, it signifies Simon's efforts being recognised and a sense of accomplishment in achievements. Looking across to the seventh card the Two of Cups provides more information that this appears to be regarding a loving, close relationship.

The most recent past, or situation that would just be passing through, the Four of Pentacles, can indicate being careful not to hold back too much emotionally. "Nothing ventured, nothing gained."

The card in the crowning thoughts revealed in position five is the Ace of Cups—also our timing card. The Ace shows that Simon's thoughts at this time will be on a whole new beginning emotionally, or a sense of renewal in the relationship. Card nine, the Three of Cups, signifies emotional growth in the relationship. With the Ace, Two, and Three of Cups all occupying the placements that represent different variations of the seeker's attitude, we can see that Simon should be feeling fairly upbeat and positive about everything. Fortunately, the rest of the reading also shows that this isn't a case of seeing things through a false rosy glow, (sometimes this can happen if the seeker is out of tune with what is happening around them.)

In the immediate future, the Emperor shows material and emotional stability through using logic and leadership abilities, placing Simon in a strong position.

I am often asked what it means when a positive card appears in a position that can be considered negative, insomuch as it represents the seeker's apprehensions. This is a classic case of really wanting something but also being worried that it may not transpire. The Two of Cups informs Simon that all should be well, symbolising the close unity of a very harmonious relationship. Being a positive card in a negative placement also emphasises his need to focus on this outcome, as against his fear that it will not.

For the second time we have another court card in the environmental position. The Queen of Cups in this position shows that this person may be instrumental in some way, as she must feel strongly to appear in this placement. With the description given Simon informed me that this sounded like a member of his partner's family, who so far had been very supportive to the existing friendship and sympathetic to his partner's struggles regarding hiding his sexual preference from the family.

We could not have asked for a better card than the Sun in the final placement, with its message of success, warmth, and a contented, happy relationship. Together with the Ace of Cups it also provided us with the timing. The final card is numbered so we take nineteen from the Sun down to a single digit. So, 1+9=10 and 1+0= 1. The first week from the beginning of March would be an important date for this relationship. It does not necessarily mean that it will be six months before the relationship begins, although this could be the case, the best that we can provide is that it will be important in some way.

This is a very positive spread showing the potential of what could lie ahead for Simon, but we cannot rule out that he will still experience the messages received from the earlier spreads first, and would need to follow their guidance in order to attain these final results. The last spread does not simply rule out the previous ones, it is the continuation of the story taken once the experiences within the World are attained, and providing his actions continue down this route.

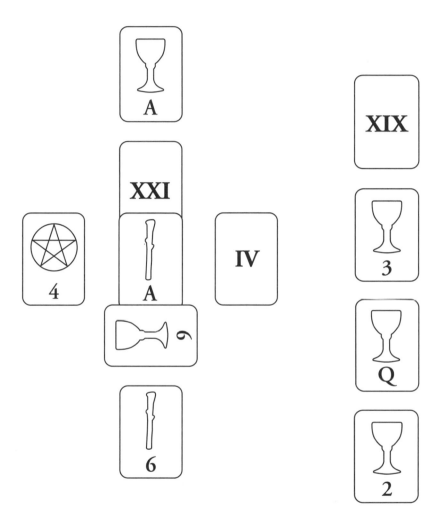

Additional Spread Summary

In summing up, I reminded Simon that everything we have been looking at represents the potentiality, or likelihood, of a situation. A great deal depends upon him and whether he takes the guidance the Tarot has provided to help him on his way. Should he decide to take an entirely different course of action, it is likely we would also be looking at a different outcome.

Whilst this is a positive reading there can sometimes be the danger of the seeker becoming over-confident in their situation. The future is not cast in stone, it fluctuates and changes based on the seeker's attitudes that drive their actions, therefore creating their future. This is why the cards can be very helpful if a negative situation can be seen, as it can help steer them through or avoid any potential difficulties that may lie ahead by changing their actions.

Results and Feedback

Four Months Later

Simon rang to let me know he had decided to sell the house he had bought. (Home area: Ten of Wands, the Moon, Six of Wands, Eight of Cups.) As much as he loved it, having created a wonderful home, he never lived there and had no inclination to move in, so it stood empty. The estate agent had been instructed to start the sale process.

At the same time he was finding the situation surrounding the relationship very hard going. Looking at the chart for the Celtic Cross spread regarding this question, I reminded him that we had the Four of Cups in the sixth position of immediate future, so it is likely he is currently experiencing this now. From his main reading it was evident that a successful outcome relied upon him nurturing the situation: this of course must remain his choice. Presently he is starting to lose hope and momentum and isn't sure he can continue. In short he said that he is "completely tired and fed-up of the status quo that exists."

Five Months Later

I received a phone call from Simon to tell me that the employee heading the new side of his business had announced she was leaving the area in a matter of weeks and therefore her position with his company. As it involved a major move he realised she must have been quietly planning this for some time. (Life Spread, work area, Key card: Ten of Swords. The Devil, Queen of Wands, Knight of Swords.) Simon reported that consequently he would be closing down this side of the business. Despite the loss of investment and subsequent failure of those plans he felt far happier for the longer-term view, as due to the economic downturn the successful side of his business had been supporting the new one financially, adding pressure to his main business. Overall he was happy to cut his losses, feeling quite relieved and more optimistic that the additional financial burden on his otherwise successful business would be removed (the Anchor, work area: the Sun).

Six Months Later

The week before the timing given in Simon's Celtic Cross, his partner suffered a bereavement. Simon rallied round to do whatever he could to be helpful and supportive. However, he told me that it was within this situation that he realised he was constantly the supportive one in the relationship and he thought there was little likelihood of this changing. He felt his partner lurched from one crisis to another and he didn't want to spend his life constantly having to bolster him up. It made him realise he wanted a relationship with a partner who would equally support him when he most needed it too. When he spoke to me he said he had realised the accuracy of the cards in the way the situation had presented itself, but his realisation came as he recognised that the aspect of the Empress, as the card of nurturing and mothering, would always be an important role he would need to play in the relationship for it to work. At the outset he had felt he would have given anything to have this relationship but once it was within his grasp the reality of what it really was, and his role within it, was not what he wanted at all. He made his choice in that moment to let the relationship go.

In Simon's Own Words

"I found my readings to be a hundred per cent accurate, they fell into place with good timings too. Through the reading I felt more focussed, clearheaded and so motivated to give me the drive to reach my goals. After I read my reading back to myself, I realised how much I have changed as a person (for the better I may add) and found I have achieved a more grounded lifestyle and learnt to take a step back and try and understand more fully the situation in hand. I felt at ease with Josie, she understood my lifestyle and what was going on in my life without being judgemental yet always professional."

Reader's Tips
Court Cards and Same-Gender Relationships

I have occasionally been asked if I use opposite gender cards to represent the partner in same gender relationships. As you can see from Simon's reading, I use the kings to represent men and queens to represent women, regardless of their sexual persuasion. Since we all have a mixture of male and female energy I feel it helps to be specific, particularly when the court cards can be an area new readers struggle with.

Similarly, just as we all share a number of characteristics from each of the suit elements representing the kings and queens, there is usually one that is more dominant. Once another person (or more) is revealed by the seeker to play a significant role in their situation it can be helpful to spend some time outlining the four different personality types for that gender, so there is no doubt once that court card appears who it may relate to. In Simon's case, once I was aware his main concern covered one person in a relationship situation, I briefly covered the different types to agree upon a court card for him and his partner. As you will note, there were no male court cards evident in the Life Spread, however it was useful before we started the Celtic Cross readings.

3

The Business Owner

I had never read for Jane before. She had only ever had one Tarot reading when she was much younger and remembers very little about it now. Jane is in her late thirties, married with two children, and she runs her own business.

First Impressions

- Judgement repeated in the Life Spread and the Anchor.
- Spreads appear work-oriented.
- The reading appears to move about—not smooth flowing. Note the Queen of Wands in first position.

Following this Reading

This reading is quite consistent with Queen of Wands types. As you will discover, this is Jane's court card. I have had several friends who have been the Queen of Wands and the one common denominator, I have discovered, is that reading for them is reflective of their very busy lifestyles—all over the place. For this reason the reading moved about from one area to another, so it is a little difficult for me to try and section it off for you and you will notice that we bounce back and forth a bit. However, if you have the cards laid out before you (which I would recommend), you will be able to make the relevant connections more easily.

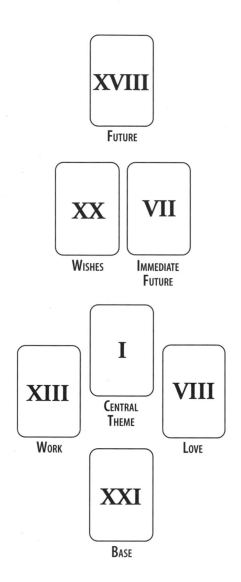

The Business Owner—Life Spread

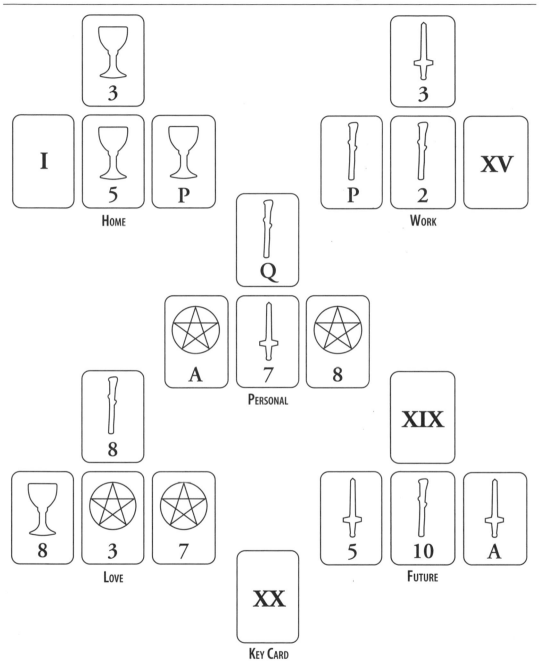

I felt it also served as a good example of a reading for a Queen of Wands. Sometimes these can literally jump from one card to the next as a different part of their life in the same outlined area, since the edges often get blurred as they dash from one thing to another. In reality, they often appear more manic than this one. Don't be put off when faced with these types, it can just take a little longer to establish facts and gel the reading.

The Anchor
BASE POSITION: THE WORLD

The World as the first card in the Anchor showed that Jane should be feeling well pleased with her accomplishments and these were probably not something that had been gained overnight but worked towards attainment. Jane confirmed this was correct.

The Life Spread
PERSONAL AREA: QUEEN OF WANDS, ACE OF PENTACLES,
SEVEN OF SWORDS, EIGHT OF PENTACLES

Moving straight across to the card in the first position of the Life Spread, I wanted to confirm the identity of the Queen of Wands represented and from the personality description we concluded that it was Jane's own card. (Always busy and on the go with a tendency to take on too much but always cheerful and optimistic.)

The Ace of Pentacles represents the founding of a new business with good potential or it could show important documents, such as contracts, house deeds, or bank accounts. I explained to Jane that with the spread I was using it was important for me to establish where we were in the time line of events in her life, so my questions were to try and identify whether some of the cards related to recent past or present situations, not the need for a full rundown of everything she may be experiencing in her life. Once this is established then we move forward, left to right, as if in a sentence to see how the situation could develop.

The Ace of Pentacles connected on both levels. A number of months previously she had set up a new branch of her business, different to the one she ran for the last number of years, in the same field but in a slightly different direction. However, as her business is connected to property, all the different types of documents I mentioned constantly surround her.

I mentioned to Jane that from the spread it seemed to show that work spilled over into the various areas of her life, because it appeared in the personal and love area as well. She agreed this was certainly the case since her husband had now joined her in the business and they were busy with their latest venture.

The Anchor
WORK AREA: DEATH
The Life Spread
WORK AREA: THREE OF SWORDS, PAGE OF WANDS,
TWO OF WANDS, THE DEVIL

The Death card in the work area seemed to represent the ending of one way of doing business and instigating a major change. Jane informed me that they had previously been in property development and owned a number of properties which they let; this led to property management and more recently, following the credit crunch, they had taken on formal premises for property letting and sales services. Another interesting aspect is that her husband had given up a good job to join her in the business, just prior to the credit crunch hitting the UK. A worrying time for anyone involved in the property market.

Before continuing with the personal area, I moved across to the Three of Swords in the work area, and asked Jane if there had been any kind of fallout or quarrel connected to the business which had (most likely) already happened. Jane said there had been no fallout internally but there had been a situation with a tradesman connected to the property development side that had been quite traumatic for them.

The Page of Wands indicated there had been some good news at work recently. Jane confirmed that since they opened their new office work had really taken off so they were now looking to relocate into premises that were better positioned. They had recently been informed of premises that were available and were in the process of obtaining the correct planning permission so they could move. This information could also further connect with the Ace of Pentacles, as the planning permission documents would come under this card.

The Two of Wands represents moving forward with the initial stages having progressed and focus now upon future plans. This positive card shows Jane moving in the direction of her goals and, interestingly enough, is often a card that can represent business partnerships. The Devil here tends to warn against overworking and becoming bogged down by the business. Jane said that because they love what they do they discovered that they talk about it nonstop, and have to make the effort not to do so at home, as they felt it wasn't fair to the children. She also said that if they didn't make a concerted effort she could easily see how work would take over and then suddenly not be quite so enjoyable. Jane felt it was an appropriate warning for her, since she did have the tendency to take on too much.

The Life Spread
PERSONAL AREA

Moving back to the personal area: the Ace of Pentacles could represent the new business, but it might also symbolise the planning documents currently going through. With the Eight of Pentacles at the end, it seems to show that they will continue to build their business, but the Seven of Swords tended to indicate that there could be an unexpected twist as to how they get there, or that diplomacy and careful handling may be required in some aspect of their business. It almost represents a hiccup in the proceedings but appears to be nothing more serious than this. Jane said they had been informed that there shouldn't be any problems with the planning application but, whichever way the cards played out, she felt relieved that it showed them continuing to build the business.

The Life Spread
LOVE AREA: EIGHT OF WANDS, EIGHT OF CUPS, THREE OF PENTACLES, SEVEN OF PENTACLES
The Anchor
LOVE AREA: STRENGTH
CENTRAL POSITION: THE MAGICIAN
IMMEDIATE FUTURE: THE CHARIOT

Because further work cards were shown I moved down to the love area. The Eight of Wands, as the Key card, symbolised events moving at a swift pace, quite often following setbacks or after a time of stagnation. The Eight of Cups showed that Jane had walked away from something through disillusionment and disappointment after she had put in an enormous amount of effort and herself into it. Jane said this would be the property development side of the business which she had absolutely thrown herself into, with her husband involved part of the time as he still had his other career at the time. She had felt completely discouraged after all the time, effort, and money they had poured into the properties to find themselves caught in the onslaught of the credit crunch. Fortunately, she had already started to build the lettings and maintenance side of the business otherwise she doubted they would have got through the situation, but it had certainly made her walk away from further development of that side of the business.

I explained that the cards following were promising. The Three of Pentacles represents work that Jane has already started, is good at, and enjoys, together with a sense of achievement and recognition. The Seven of Pentacles shows continued growth, which although not necessarily fast, and represents the rewards of work coming to fruition following due care and attention being applied. Whilst the Seven also brings financial improvement, it advises that work will still have to be done towards the future in order to provide further rewards.

In the centre of the Anchor, the Magician lends strong support that Jane has all the skills and ability she needs to move forward, she just needs to continue to apply herself and have confidence in those abilities. So far all the indications for work and business are very good. Moving through the various areas, the Two of Wands shows looking towards future growth and plans, the Eight of Pentacles continuing to develop the business, the Three and Seven of Pentacles, as just mentioned. So the only warning here is really to ensure that Jane doesn't allow herself to become bogged down in business and overwork—which the Devil shows is self-inflicted—and then feel chained to the business. Half the battle with the Devil card is to recognise the situation before it fully develops into an obsession or addiction, so seeing the signs provides a good warning to ensure Jane doesn't fall into this trap. Jane said the reading so far sounded "spot on" and she could identify with all that was being said.

In the love area we have Strength, an extremely good card to have in this area, suggesting that Jane's relationship is filled with gentle qualities and inner strength, providing determination to actively achieve their goals together and to make the relationship work. Jane confirmed this sounded exactly right. As this card is already being experienced, I told her this would continue into the future.

In the immediate future, the Chariot informs Jane to keep her energies focussed in one direction and not allow them to become scattered, so that she may achieve her goals. As a card of determination, it also represents triumph over obstacles, so she has the ability to overcome whatever might come into her path, even if the ride seems bumpy at times.

The Life Spread
HOME AREA: THREE OF CUPS, THE MAGICIAN,
FIVE OF CUPS, PAGE OF CUPS

Moving back to the Life Spread, the Three of Cups in the home area shows progressive growth in the relationship, a happy card, perhaps suggesting celebrations recently, but tending to show an abundance of love at home. I asked if there had been any family celebrations recently and Jane said her parents had celebrated their fiftieth wedding anniversary this year. She told me that she felt very lucky in her personal life and that home was a happy place, filled with love. Again, with the Magician it tends to suggest work spilling into the home area. This is not really a surprise now since we know that husband and wife work together in business, and there are enough indications to show that the marriage and family life are strong, so it is not a concern.

The Five of Cups following the Magician indicates feelings of being let down and seems at odds in this area, so I asked Jane if there been had any regrets over past actions recently, or if she had felt badly let down by someone? Jane said that she felt that way about the trades-man and they felt very hurt over it (Three of Swords in the work area), as it was a situation they had never encountered before and was someone they originally knew on a personal level and trusted. Having let them down badly he then issued legal proceedings, which was a major surprise as he hadn't discussed the issue with them first. Consequently, Jane and her husband took legal advice and immediately counter-claimed, as they had lost money through his initial actions and felt they had not done anything wrong.

I informed Jane that I found this interesting because there were no legal cards showing, although the Page of Cups indicated that they should receive some good news concerning this that they would be happy about. Jane said their solicitor had informed them that the tradesman wasn't co-operating by responding or providing necessary information, and so she had suggested contacting him and settling the matter out of court. As Jane could identify with the cards it seemed most likely that this was the area being covered, particularly since it had been such a big event for them, was ongoing and there were no legal cards present. However, just to be on the safe side, I advised her that if this wasn't the situation then there could be a feeling of let-down still to come, although this needed to be kept in proportion as to how it was shown. I was quick to point out that the card was quite isolated, that it was followed by good news and some of the key words in this card are "a feeling of," which is how the card affects people. If this were the case, it would somehow be connected to the home area, such as a friend or family member, but appeared short-lived with a happy outcome. The important thing here was to see it all in context.

The Life Spread
THE KEY CARD: JUDGEMENT
The Anchor
WISHES: JUDGEMENT

With Judgement repeated in both spreads the name itself seems very apt and quite literal to the pending legal situation she has now informed me about, although I have never associated this card with actual judgements being made, legal or otherwise, so I was curious to know how Jane related to it.

I explained that the card in the wishes area often reflects what a person most wishes for but often isn't visible to others externally. Since it is also the Key card of the Life Spread it clearly held some importance, and I hoped she would be able to throw some light on it. I explained that Judgement often shows revival or renewal; as a card of resurrection it tends to liberate us from past experiences, wiser and ready to move forward. It can represent reconciliation with someone from the past or something from the past renewed. "As you sow, so shall you reap," the results of the seeds you have previously planted.

Jane felt that Judgement represented the learning path they had encountered through their business, the awful experience of having worked hard and put everything on the line, and then watching with horror as the property market plunged. Thankfully, they had already branched out into associated areas, leaving them less vulnerable. Jane hoped their hard work would pay off and that in time the values of their initial expenditure would return. Meanwhile, she recognised that had it not been for this experience they would not be doing what they are now, and that they were very much enjoying the new part of their business.

The Life Spread
THE FUTURE: THE SUN, FIVE OF SWORDS, TEN OF WANDS, ACE OF SWORDS

The overall theme with the future is success, shown by the Sun as the main card; the Ace of Swords at the end of the reading provides triumph over adversity. This is helpful, since the Five of Swords and Ten of Wands suggest that there may be a few bumps en route. Now that I am aware of it, it is difficult to tell whether the Five of Swords may relate back to the legal situation, as there is always the risk of hanging everything onto what you are already aware of, otherwise it is a warning to be watchful of people with a hidden agenda, or those who may not have Jane's best interests at heart. This could be connected to things we have covered in the reading or it might be a situation quite on its own. The Ten of Wands could show that this would make her feel weighed down at the time, but the Ace of Swords tells us that she will ultimately win through.

The Ten of Wands also echoes the Devil in the work area, being careful of not taking on too much and then feeling overburdened. The Ace of Swords is an excellent card to complete the reading, I always consider this card a godsend, rather like the proverbial "ace up the sleeve," or the adage, "if life gives you lemons then you make lemonade!" No matter what the situation, so long as you are prepared to put in the effort, with this Ace on your side you will come through eventually. Jane said their success so far had been in this mould, hard work was not a problem so long as they felt they were heading in the right direction.

Finally, the Moon at the end of the Anchor is an interesting card to finish the reading, in the future position and with the other indications I feel it is a warning of not making any decisions too quickly. By the light of the moon nothing can appear quite as it is in daylight, creating shapes in the shadows that disappear once the lights are switched on. The Moon suggests there is more going on under the surface than she is aware of, so it is wise to let the facts emerge before making decisions even if it is just sleeping on them overnight. It may also be advising Jane to take a slightly more cautious approach than she has in the past. Overall there are good indications in the reading with a few cautionary notes running throughout, so I felt that the Moon seemed to crystallise that information.

FOLLOWING THE THREAD

Jane's story gradually unfolded as the reading progressed and since the situation with the tradesman was so heavy in her mind I felt most of this reading probably related to it. Whichever area we look at, it seems to keep cropping up. As we have now been told this is a potential legal case, so quite serious, it should perhaps be no surprise that elements of this would filter in throughout the different areas of her Life Spread. Overall, it appears like a dark cloud that hangs over them on an otherwise bright landscape.

However, for me the interesting thing is that there are no legal cards here and no loss showing. Given the seriousness of the matter, and if it were to go badly, I would expect to see quite different cards. Instead, if we consider what is now known, it is possible that we are being shown a repeated message throughout in the various areas.

The Seven of Swords (personal area) the careful handling of something—could the Ace of Pentacles also be the issued legal papers demanding payment? It sometimes represents an important document of material relevance but the Eight of Pentacles shows the continuation of building her business.

The Three of Swords in the work area as the Key card, which highlighted the fallout but again, the Page of Wands and Two of Wands show continuation. Now I wonder if the Devil may also relate to how bogged down they feel about the pending legal problem, although I do feel the overworking aspect is still being warned.

In the home area we have the disappointment from someone who was a personal friend (the Five of Cups) but it is followed by good news. In the immediate future the Five of Swords may show further underhandedness and feeling overwhelmed by the situation from the Ten of Wands, but positive energy from the Sun and Ace of Swords literally sandwich these cards, hemming them in. This should reduce their impact, particularly since it is a major and an ace, also the Sun being the most positive in the Tarot and the interpretation found in the Ace of Swords. The Moon at the end of the Anchor may also represent the hidden information yet to be disclosed.

Taking everything into account that Jane has revealed it is evident that their life is quite uncomplicated and otherwise for the most part, happy and settled. I feel that most of the disruptive elements of the reading stem from and relate to the potential legal case showing itself. With the Magician as her central card in the Anchor and all the other indications showing, including those cards relevant by their absence, I am sure they will see a good outcome and I cannot say I see a court case here, or the financial devastation losing the case would bring.

Additional Spread: Celtic Cross

I asked Jane if there was anything further she would like to ask the Tarot. Whilst she felt that the reading had covered everything, she did want to know if the cards would provide any more information on the pending legal situation. I covered the four different personality types of the Kings with Jane first, so we would recognise the tradesman's court card if it appeared in the reading. The King of Cups was chosen.

The cards from the Life Spread were gathered, placed back into the full deck, and handed to Jane for shuffling. All the while, she was to concentrate on the question: Would they resolve the dispute with (his name) in their favour? The cards were then cut into three, as usual, collected, and lain out.

In the present position I felt the Lovers represented Jane and her husband, lovers and business partners with a very strong, close bond. The Nine of Wands crossing the situation as the

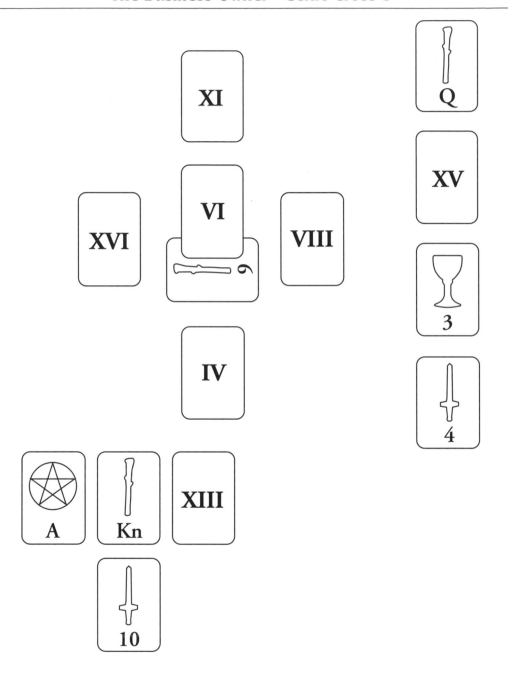

"filter" card symbolised the situation very well, with the Wands behind the figure signifying all that Jane and her husband had worked hard for and now defending their position. Although weary with the matter it shows a good deal of determination and courage to stand up for themselves in the counter claim. With the Emperor providing further information to our first card we can see that the decision they came to was realised with rationale and logic, which led them to take the initiative.

The fourth card reveals the recent past and the Tower was most accurate as to how events had happened with the shock and loss that had resulted. (Unfortunately, as it covers a third party and was quite in-depth, I cannot disclose all the details I was given by Jane in the Life Spread regarding the dispute.) It is always encouraging for the seeker when the first cards cover everything so well, as it lends more confidence to the rest of the reading.

Justice, as Jane's crowning thoughts, relates to the pending legal action and balanced thought in dealing with the matter. Looking across at her hopes and wishes in position nine, we can see from the Devil that she is feeling quite bogged down by the situation. With two major cards balanced across from one another in these positions we can see that they both have equal hold on the way she feels about it.

As the name suggests, Strength in position six of the immediate future provides courage, strength, and endurance in order to achieve desired results. The Four of Swords in the appre-hensions position shows us a period of rest and recovery following strain; gathering together all the resources needed before picking up the sword to fight again, figuratively speaking. This matches well, balanced across from the Emperor (position 3) with his logic and leadership, also two fours, a number of stability, providing a further mini-cameo within the history.

Since the person was named in the question, card eight represents how he is/will be view-ing the situation. We also need to look at the tenth card here, so as not to be misled, for whilst the Three of Cups symbolises celebrations in the eighth position we can see that ultimately the answer is associated with, or relies upon, the Queen of Wands. This could be Jane as it is her own card but alternatively it could be another lady who shares similar characteristics. Although I would find this unusual, as the cards would normally show a different court card to represent someone else, it is still a possibility. Jane pointed out that her solicitor was similar to herself, so it may be through her actions. However, I would have expected the Queen of Swords to show as her solicitor and ultimately she would recommend actions to her client but it would remain their decision, so the likelihood is that it is Jane's own card.

As the immediate future and the outcome must both be ultimately connected, with Strength it tends to show how this will be resolved by Jane, perhaps by her decision or her actions in the process. From the cards present I felt that the dispute would be resolved to everyone's satisfaction, technically a win-win situation. Jane said she felt this was possible if the tradesman accepted the recent proposal of an offer to settle out of court, as if the case went ahead it would be expensive for both parties and the "win" for either side would therefore be quite small. With the two cards in positions six and ten, and with Strength in the immediate future, I felt there could still be some negotiations to take place in order to arrive at the conclusion and the result therefore, depended upon how it was handled by the Queen of Wands. I also reminded Jane of the Moon card in her future position in the Anchor, informing her to take her time in making decisions, ensuring all the facts were at hand first because they could still be emerging.

The cards in the Reader's Fan provided backup to the history of the situation, with the Ace of Pentacles as the original contracts for the work. The Knight of Wands sometimes symbolises property and the contracted work had involved a property conversion. Death and the Ten of Swords provide further information regarding the sudden end of the work and the business relationship, together with the ruined plans and resulting disappointment.

Jane said the reading was "absolutely spot-on" regarding everything that was going on around them and felt it had been very helpful and encouraging, given their previous year and with the new business they were building. She also felt it had picked up "fantastically well" on the overworking situation, of not allowing themselves to become overburdened or encroach into their home and family time, as they had in the past, because they love what they do so much.

Results and Revisit

Six Weeks Later

Jane rang me to let me know they had received the change of use planning consent and were now operating from their new business premises.

Two-and-a-Half Months Later

With exactly two weeks to go before the court case, Jane's nerves are getting the better of her. The tradesman is still pursuing the case and she wants to know if I would mind doing

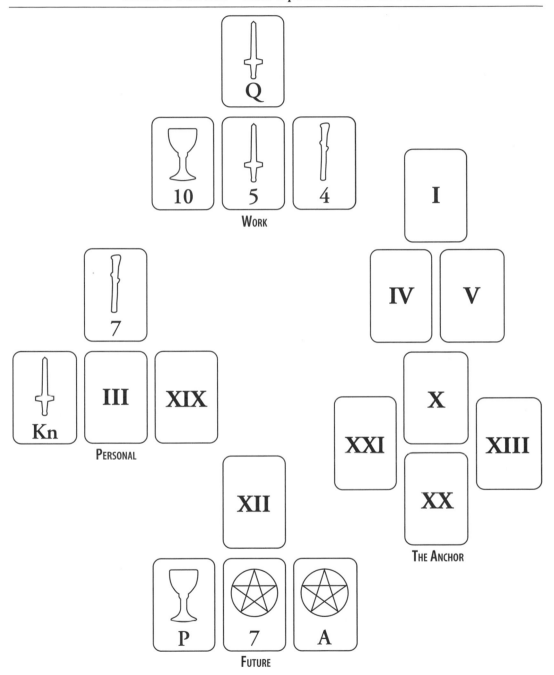

another reading for her. I ask if there have been any further developments since we last met and she informs me that there have, so we arrange to meet.

Although her only concern is the court case and her main answer could probably be found in a single Celtic Cross, I still lay out the Life Spread and Anchor first as it provides a broader overview and ensures I don't miss something important that may have developed. In order not to lengthen this case study too much, and for the purpose of the book, I will relate only the areas of the Life Spread that were relevant for the situation. Although the cards for the home and love areas were slightly different, the messages were consistent to those given previously.

As we are already fully aware of all the circumstances surrounding Jane's situation, I am hoping you find these cards leaping out from the page at you, perhaps even more so if you have taken a moment to lay out the cards in front of you.

The Anchor

Looking at the Anchor it almost feels as if we could simply read this as a connecting chain, it flows so smoothly. The Judgement card in the present position highlights the matter with roots in the past now being resurrected, and although the interpretation I use doesn't follow its namesake I am amazed at the reappearance of this appropriately named card!

I took Death in the love area to represent a definite ending of the unpleasant situation surrounding Jane and her husband, since it has been such a major factor in their lives and because they are also business partners.

The World in the work area is very encouraging with its message of assured success and completion of a cycle. The Wheel of Fortune is the central card for the reading and shows good fortune is on their side, with a new chapter of luck about to commence. The Hierophant could be the higher authorities of the law institution.

The Emperor in Jane's wishes position appeared to show her resolve had also strengthened, whilst also amplifying their desire to see the application of logical thought applied with authority. Jane informs me that they have now seen witness statements and paperwork from the other side and feel more confident. Although they do not doubt their position is good they are still concerned as to whether the court will see the truth and rule in their favour. Jane reminds me they have never had legal action taken against them and the idea of actually going to court makes her feel physically sick.

The Magician also bodes well for the future, informing Jane to actively apply her talents with confidence, concentration, and willpower, and that she already has the skills and ability required to handle a task well and bring it to a successful conclusion.

Having leapt ahead slightly, let's see how this connects with the Life Spread.

The Life Spread
PERSONAL AREA: SEVEN OF WANDS, KNIGHT OF SWORDS, THE EMPRESS, THE SUN

As the first card of the reading, the Seven of Wands reflects Jane feeling challenged to defend her position. This card usually affects people on a fundamental level, since it may feel as if their core beliefs are under fire, the foundations of their principles. Jane agreed they felt it was more a fight regarding their honesty and principles being at stake rather than the money involved, although the sums were substantial.

With the Knight of Swords I asked Jane if there had been some fairly rapid activity recently, perhaps surrounded by a sense of chaos. She felt this card was also very accurate and went on to explain that a different solicitor within the practice had been passed their file; he had rang them after close of business whilst they were in the car. She said he was highly efficient and quite stern, bombarding her husband with questions, a list of instructions and answers he wanted. They had been in the car for a long time and her husband said he felt shell-shocked by the end of it. He immediately had to set to work providing a highly detailed statement, which resulted in a document of fifty-three pages. Jane said it was as if everything suddenly started to happen with an enormous sense of urgency.

The Empress and the Sun complete this area beautifully, two positive major cards with a repeated message of success and reinforcing one another. Reading as a thread they show success through nurturing; care and attention leads to the success contained from the Sun, which brings a happy outcome. (This said, I have already scanned all the other relevant areas before making this statement…just in case!)

The Life Spread
WORK AREA: QUEEN OF SWORDS, TEN OF CUPS, FIVE OF SWORDS, FOUR OF WANDS
The Anchor
WORK AREA: THE WORLD

The Queen of Swords is usually a strong and forthright woman and, as she can be connected to law, I ask Jane if there is a female solicitor involved with them. Jane cannot place this lady. They had previously dealt with a female solicitor (before being passed across to the male solicitor currently dealing with them), but she was newly qualified and Jane didn't feel she fit the personality given. As the Key card for this area the Queen of Swords appeared to be important in some way, so I asked Jane to be watchful for her appearance.

The Five of Swords is sandwiched between two positive cards. They are all minor and whilst the Ten of Cups and Four of Wands seem to squash the Five it makes me think its appearance sours the situation, but because it is hemmed in with positive influences its effect appears nullified. Had the Five of Swords been the last card of the group it would have read differently. Reading them progressively, from left to right, the Ten of Cups may seem odd in this area, but Jane and her husband are in business together, so home and work are intertwined and they are happy and content with their life. The Five of Swords perhaps represents the underhandedness of how the dealings arose surrounding the dispute, resulting in the claim made against them, which they strongly contest. The energy of this card could still be at play, so there may be some further incidents yet to follow, although with the Four of Wands following and the way the card is hemmed in, I feel this is unlikely. The Four can represent people celebrating together, a period of rest and enjoyment following their labours, also a sense of stability.

The Life Spread
FUTURE AREA: THE HANGING MAN, PAGE OF CUPS, SEVEN OF PENTACLES, ACE OF PENTACLES

The three minor cards below read well together but I have difficulty placing the Hanging Man as the Key card. The Page of Cups brings messages of an emotional nature; with positive cards following the usual interpretation that this is happy news seems right. The Seven of Pentacles brings the rewards of one's diligent labours, the harvest about to be collected, and a good indicator for any financial dealings.

Together with the Ace of Pentacles, which can also represent lump sums of money but also important documents with a material connection, this line looks very promising. Does the Hanging Man mean there will be some kind of sacrifice made in the shorter term for a greater benefit in the future? And, if so, does that mean Jane and her husband will be making a concession in some way here? Alternatively, is it the claimant who makes the sacrifice and still steps down? Since the case is only two weeks away, and with all the other cards we have, it does not appear to mean "life in suspension."

This leaves me with another option I would use with this card, observing matters from a different standpoint in order to find a better understanding. Considering what has happened perhaps it leads to a more enlightened view for Jane and her husband on how they operate in future. With their experience of having placed trust in a friend and therefore foregone some of the more contractual arrangements, it may be an experience they will never repeat. I'm not sure with this card and don't feel I can provide anything further. However, with all the other indications, including the majors in the Anchor, I feel Jane is still looking at a positive outcome, and more certain than in her previous reading from two and a half months ago.

Revisit: Celtic Cross

The Life Spread is gathered up, Jane shuffles the deck, this time concentrating on her question of whether they will win the court case against the person (whom she names.)

Looking back to my charts from Jane's visit it is interesting that the Lovers was in the first position then too! I feel the Lovers in the first position represents Jane and her husband and the choices they have faced leading up to the legal case—of course, they also have the choice of backing out of the case before it goes to court. The filter, or atmosphere, of the reading is good with the Wheel of Fortune.

The High Priestess, as the history to the first card, informs us there have been secrets revealed that have been to their benefit. Jane tells me that since certain documents have now had to be released to them a number of issues have stood out as being incorrect and for which they have reliable witnesses. This has reinforced their choice (from the Lovers card) to continue with the case.

The Death card in the most recent past, which is also repeated in the Anchor, shows a definite ending to the matter—as this hasn't yet happened it should manifest within the next two weeks. (Surprisingly enough, the court case is exactly two weeks to the day of this reading.)

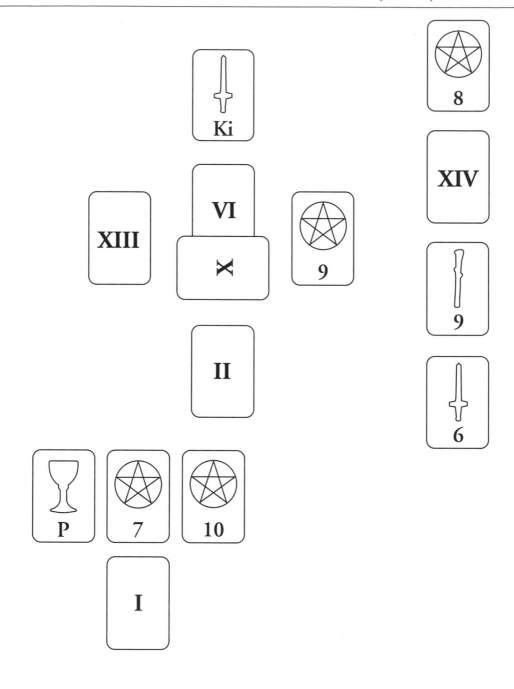

Is the King of Swords in Jane's crowning thoughts their new solicitor? Balanced across from Temperance he should have inspired more balanced emotions, found in the message of this card. Jane says they feel much happier and more confident since they have been dealing with him.

In the immediate future the Nine of Pentacles should bring some financial gain, and with this card it is usually from their own efforts—so an excellent card for this placement.

In Jane's apprehensions the Six of Swords reveals her desire to move forward and away from this stressful time, together with cards 5 and 9 we see she has a good attitude in tune with the rest of the reading.

I found the Nine of Wands really helpful here, since she had named the person, so it represents how he views the situation. On the one hand it could be taken that he is viewing them as boldly defending their position and refusing to give up but I also felt it suggested he was becoming rather battle-weary with the matter as well. From the original reading, and given what Jane has now said about the errors in statements, I am still surprised he hasn't pulled out yet.

With all the other indications in the reading, and with the Nine of Pentacles in some way having a direct link to the Eight of Pentacles, my immediate thought was "business as usual." Jane and her husband are still developing their business, so this fits in with the apprenticeship interpretation found with this card. Whilst they would continue with their business even if they lost the case, the financial costs would be large and could place a strain on them, but the Nine of Pentacles appeared to improve their financial situation, which would help them to continue more easily.

The Reader's Fan brings us some repeated messages and reinforced the reading for me. It reads directly and smoothly, one card to the next. Good news they are happy with concerning money and property and proceeding with confidence.

Given all the cards we have seen in the spreads I tell Jane I am sure they will not lose their case, and if it proceeds I feel it will go in their favour in court, although I still feel it is possible that the claimant may pull out. Either way, this should leave them in a winning position. However, I remind her it is extremely important that they follow the legal advice they are being provided with.

Jane says she feels the reading has been very beneficial and although she knows she will still worry about going to court she feels more confident and less worried about the outcome.

Revisit: Results and Feedback
Three Months After the Original Reading

The tradesman pulled out two days before the court case. Jane said they had only met the barrister representing them in court shortly before, but she was female and "absolutely ferocious," which made her think this was the Queen of Swords referred to in her last reading. Jane said that once the details of such a good case were available to the other side, together with the knowledge of their barrister's identity, this might have been enough to make the other side withdraw!

When I asked how this outcome would affect everyone financially Jane told me it meant that each side would just pay their own costs. Jane and her husband are pleased with the outcome and much relieved that they can get on with life without the constant worry hanging over them.

In Jane's Own Words

At the time of the readings the personal worry and stress of being in a situation of going to court, with the outcome unknown, I can only describe (without being seen to be dramatic) as horrendous!

The readings, as a result of the cards, could not have been more encouraging and did give me a balanced view of a tricky situation, with good advice for proceeding with caution and sleeping on issues, both for the pending court case and our business and personal lives.

The detail of the card indications was outstanding. Having re-read the readings I can say hand on heart how appropriate and spot on they were. When I came away from the readings and repeated back what the cards said to my husband I felt more hopeful and encouraged that the outcome would be a positive one for us personally. I certainly slept better the night of the last reading.

As for the Queen of Swords, what an interesting lady she turned out to be, in the form of our barrister, not someone we would have liked to face across the court!

In summary, did the readings make a difference to me? Absolutely, they empowered and guided me to carry on and see it through. I felt an immense sense that it would be all right.

Reader's Tips
Absent Cards

One of the noticeable aspects of Jane's reading was the absent cards. Sometimes the answers to our questions can be found not only by what is present but also by what is not. In this instance there were no legal cards or loss represented. In the summary at the end of Jane's first main reading, all the indications showed continuation of their business but those that would represent hardship or loss were not evident.

This can work both ways, in the positive and the negative. Someone looking for the happy ending in an existing relationship may have a solitary Ten of Cups yet not produce the solidity of more required cards to suggest commitment and permanency (marriage.) Alternatively, the person who fears they face a split or divorce in their relationship may show cards that reveal niggles and challenges but those that bring final endings are missing. It provides us with the ability to show the seeker the prevalent energy surrounding a situation that they may be working with, or against, at least in the immediate foreseeable future.

All the cards tell a story, sometimes even by their noticeable absence. At times it can be a fine line … as we will see in the next case study.

Frequency of Consultations

Another reason for asking if someone has had a Tarot reading before, aside from being helpful regarding any preconceptions they may have, is that it can alert you to someone who may have become addicted to consulting readers. Since we view Tarot readings as empowering for the seeker we do not want to unwittingly create a situation where they become too reliant on the cards for everyday decisions, or transfer the responsibility they take in their own life. If you book your appointments by telephone it can provide the opportunity to ask this question prior to making the booking.

As a general rule, if I have read for someone recently and they contact me for another reading within a short timeframe I will only read for them if there has been a change of circumstances, or where a new set of events may have come into the equation. Instances of this have included: steering a business through a difficult time, awkward and ongoing negotiations, developments through the stages of divorce, or for instance, if they consulted me due to career concerns but then encounter a relationship issue.

My own rule of thumb is that follow-ups to developing situations that may have become more pressing are acceptable, but if they want to book with me constantly concerning the same issues when there have been no changes then I will decline. In those cases I would politely explain that if nothing has occurred to change the circumstances then the likelihood is that the cards will repeat the original information, until the results we discussed have come to fruition. On that basis it would be better to return later or when they have a different situation, and then I would be happy to read for them again. By taking this approach most people have thanked me for being honest with them. Sometimes they just have concerns or need the reassurance of a few gentle words.

Whether or not you charge for your readings it is still your time and it remains your prerogative to decline a reading if you do not feel comfortable for any reason. Remember that it's your call.

4
The Former Model

*L*aura had a number of readings with me a few years ago when she was just breaking into the world of modelling. Her cards had been very accurate concerning her initial success in that industry and the people she met who were influential to her. Fast forward a few years and she has left the modelling world behind. Laura is in her twenties, has recently started a new business partnership, and is married with two children.

First Impressions

- The Devil, High Priestess, and Five of Swords in the work area.
- Three Fives in three separate areas of the Life Spread.
- Wheel of Fortune repeated in both spreads.
- The Fool in the wishes area of the Anchor.

The Anchor
BASE POSITION: THE WHEEL OF FORTUNE

The Wheel of Fortune in the starting position made a positive start to the reading and pointed to a run of luck with a new chapter of life commencing. I asked Laura if she could associate with this and if it represented what had happened in her life recently. Laura said she felt this was true of her life overall and that was exactly how it felt, like a whole new chapter, as there

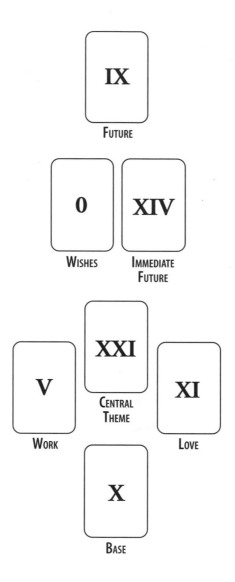

The Former Model—Life Spread

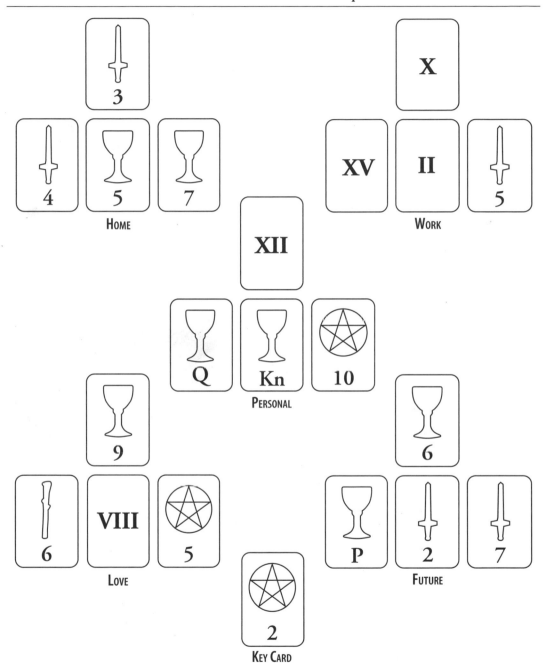

had been many changes within the last year and certainly over the last few months. This had involved moving home, opening the business, and positive changes in her marriage.

The Anchor
WORK AREA: THE HIEROPHANT
The Life Spread
**WORK AREA: WHEEL OF FORTUNE, THE DEVIL,
THE HIGH PRIESTESS, FIVE OF SWORDS**

I referred to the Wheel of Fortune also in her work area of the Life Spread but didn't expand on this yet because of the three cards below. I checked the work area of the Anchor first to see if I could see a link or more information to connect the three cards below. The Hierophant can represent large institutions that have a set way of doing things, tradition and convention often feature strongly, and as I explained this to Laura I mentioned that churches fall into this category when she told me that the landlord of her business premises was a church. Because this card was in the work area of the Anchor, this was obviously going to feature strongly in some way. At this stage I moved back to the Life Spread to deal with the remaining cards.

The Wheel of Fortune sat positively at the top but it seemed detached from the other cards of the work area. The Devil can represent feeling bogged down in some way and Laura said they have had some enormous challenges with the business, including opening in a recession, and a number of serious structural problems with the building over a period of weeks, creating a lot of disruption and sleepless nights.

However, whilst this card did fit the most recent past it was the overlapping connection of secrecy with the three together that could not be missed. The Devil can be secret plans; the High Priestess shows secrets that would become known to Laura that would be to her benefit, and the Five of Swords an element of deceit or underhandedness. Whilst the cards read together as one group, the Five of Swords sits at the end (and we are always forward moving, left to right). As a minor card it holds less power than the two majors before it, but it is the last card, and the positive vibrations of the High Priestess is sandwiched by the negative energy of the other two.

I told Laura I would explain the cards to her in this area, as I saw them, and perhaps she may be able to shed some light on the situation. I then covered the cards individually, before explaining that as a group it appeared that something could be brewing at work.

Since this would be working to her disadvantage, and she could lose something (or business) through an unfair manner, I advised her to be very watchful. Another aspect of the Five is when someone suddenly leaves without proper explanation or sensitivity to others concerned. I explained that an employee leaving and taking clients, for instance, would fit these cards, but there were no court cards to identify any particular individual.

Dishonesty, deceit, and unethical dealings normally surround the Five, and although from the minor arcana, it is one of my least favourite cards. From my experience it never fails to make a show when dodgy dealings surround something and the results are normally hurtful on a personal level to the inquirer. This situation appeared fairly isolated and didn't seem to have any further effect. Keeping this in context, whilst it may be an unpleasant situation, it didn't seem to have disastrous repercussions based on the rest of the reading.

At this stage I asked what the current situation was with her landlord, the church, because we had identified them as the Hierophant in the Anchor and there must be a reason why this card would feature. Whilst there had been quite close involvement from the church recently, due to the amount of times damage had been repaired, it is still possible that there could be a further connection. Laura said that she had just found out in the last couple of weeks that her premises were going to be sold to a new landlord. I suggested that it might be worth asking her solicitor to double check the details of her lease agreement, just to ensure that she was adequately protected from any changes that may result. It seemed unlikely from her description of the lease but given the three cards showing in the work area of the Life Spread it may be worth checking the finer details.

Aside from this, the Hierophant could represent a mentor, or someone she trusted providing business advice, or another large institution could feature in some way. As the Anchor is the main focal point of reference, and considering the three cards in the work area of the Life Spread, if they were connected you would expect a different major card to be showing here, such as the Devil repeated, or perhaps the Tower. The Hierophant must be relevant in some way but I can't see any further connection and it puzzles me somewhat.

The work area of the Life Spread was the only one that appeared straightforward to read. In many ways, the other areas seemed somewhat disjointed or disconnected. There appeared to be contradictions, or glitches, with three fives also showing an element of instability at play in three areas.

With Justice in the love area of the Anchor, the Three of Swords as the Key card for home, and the Nine of Cups as the Key card for love and relationships, I decided to tackle this part next.

The Anchor
Love Area: Justice
The Life Spread
Home Area: Three of Swords, Four of Swords, Five of Cups, Seven of Cups

The Three of Swords can show quarrelling, conflicts, or in some cases separation, although this doesn't always mean a permanent split. In *Easy Tarot* I cover this card a number of times, in the interpretation and examples, as it can sometimes show couples that are separated through distance due to circumstances, such as work. This was a good example, as in this instance it covered both for Laura. After a brief separation she had reunited with her husband a number of months ago, but now he has a new job, which means he works out of the country and away from home for considerable periods of time.

We took the Four of Swords to represent the period of rest and recovery after strain, following the breakup. The Five of Cups can show a sense of loss, feelings of betrayal, or regrets over past actions, and this could refer to the present situation but I did not feel entirely convinced, and feel that it may still be to come.

Inwardly I am taking in the contradictions I referred to previously. It is difficult in some ways to convey, because in writing it appears lengthy, but when doing the reading it happens in your mind very quickly. It reminds me of scenes in movies where they show highlighted letters or numbers from a group that stand out when someone is cracking some kind of code in their mind.

If you have the cards before you then you will be able to follow where I was drawn, perhaps intuitively, as they follow no particular set pattern otherwise. The Seven of Cups at the end of the home area (choices or imagination), the Five of Pentacles at the end of the love area (loss), the Knight of Cups sitting in the centre of the personal area (offers of love), the full group in the future position of the Life Spread (someone from the past; messages of an emotional nature; not knowing which way to turn; speech, talk, and diplomacy). The Hermit as the future card in the Anchor shows a time for deep contemplation. Justice in the love area of the Anchor, showing logical and balanced thought, the Hanging Man as the first card of the Life Spread and the Two of Pentacles as the Key card. In the wishes position of the Anchor we have the Fool, suggesting Laura inwardly wants something completely new and different. There are hints and suggestions here, but they don't unfold immediately, and I am aware that I don't feel completely comfortable because it seems that something isn't quite right. I have nothing more concrete to give her at the moment, so I must work through the reading with her until something slots into place or becomes more evident.

Moving across to the love area of the Anchor, Justice shows the need for a balanced mind and taking a logical approach to matters. It can also represent some form of legal documents (these could be anything relating to house, deeds etc., but would still be relevant to the relationship) and I ask Laura if any of this seems relevant at the present time. Aside from trying to be rational about the relationship, due to the recent split, she doesn't otherwise feel it applies at the moment.

With the Seven of Cups, together with Justice, I advise her that an incident may arise where her imagination could give the impression that there are lots of exciting options available to her, but in reality they may not all be what they seem. Since the Seven follows the Five of Cups there could be a danger of building castles in the air and at that time it would be wise to apply the message of the Justice card, where a logical approach will be called for. A situation could arise where Laura may feel she is faced with a number of choices connected to the relationship and feel overly optimistic about it. All I am saying is that should this occur to be careful and not allow herself to get carried away, to stop and think and try to keep her feet on the ground, because she won't be seeing everything clearly and will need to be logical.

The Life Spread
Personal Area: The Hanging Man, Queen of Cups, Knight of Cups, Ten of Pentacles

I point out to Laura that we need to be careful here because there are a number of contradictory messages in her cards, and take her to the Hanging Man in the first position in the personal area. I ask if she feels as if her life is in suspension in some way and Laura says for all that is going on around her and as busy as she is, that is precisely how she feels. Although Laura shows a lot of Queen of Wands tendencies, because of how busy she always is, she has a more sensitive nature and likes things to be aesthetically pleasing. Her business ties in with the suit of Cups and, astrologically, she is also a water sign. So we safely consider her as the Queen of Cups.

The Knight of Cups often brings offers and love invitations, although this could also be connected to property offers in some way, as the Ten of Pentacles follows it and I have often found these cards together when property transactions take place. Normally this Ten refers to the family home, or material and emotional stability in the home with strong family ties, so

I feel there is (or will be) a family connection here somewhere. Laura tells me that they were recently offered a different home but they feel very happy and settled where they are. All the cards fit the situation but it is extremely rare that I have found them all to focus only on the past, so again I feel that a situation could present itself in the future and is yet to follow.

The Life Spread
LOVE AREA: NINE OF CUPS, SIX OF WANDS, STRENGTH, FIVE OF PENTACLES

The interesting thing here is that whilst we have the Ten of Pentacles, which is usually good for material stability for the family, in the love area we have the Five of Pentacles on the end, warning to guard against loss. It seems a further contradiction. The Nine of Cups, as our Key card, in the love area points to feeling that wishes have been fulfilled and a sense of abundance. The Six of Wands can be the bearer of great news but also shows a sense of satisfaction with accomplishments, with others recognising your efforts and achievements.

Laura said these two cards really applied to their situation. Everything had turned around for them over the past year, having gone from one extreme to the other. Her husband lost his job but retrained and acquired a better one and she opened her new business. They moved home and financially things had never been so good.

The Strength card sits well here, showing inner strength and courage, applying patience and diplomacy in order to achieve the required results. It provides a good deal of feminine power to Laura in this area of her life, particularly as it is the only major card showing here. However, the Five of Pentacles appears to sit completely on its own at the end of the grouping, warning against loss. This can be emotional or financial loss, so I explain to Laura that she needs to be very careful in any future dealings, to dot the "i's" and cross the "t's" and not to take any unnecessary risks. Whilst things appear to be going well financially at the moment it could be worth having a "rainy day fund," as there could be an unexpected bill or hardship, perhaps just a bump in the road, but the Five of Pentacles usually shows a strain on finances in some way.

I recount with Laura the three fives in the three different areas of her reading, which although minor cards of a low number, can point to instability in differing ways and create an uncomfortable feeling. We have the deceit and underhandedness in the work area, regrets in the home area, and now the five of loss in the love area. In varying ways they can all be suggesting loss, but it's important to keep them in perspective to the rest of the reading. It appears as if the fives seem to act as warning signals of things to guard against, perhaps nothing more than the proverbial fly in the ointment, although my main concern is the three cards we covered in the work area.

The Life Spread
FUTURE AREA: SIX OF CUPS, PAGE OF CUPS, TWO OF SWORDS, SEVEN OF SWORDS

Moving to the future area of the Life Spread, the Six of Cups can bring something or someone back from the past and this is the main theme of the area. The Page of Cups shows messages of an emotional nature coming in, most likely connected and generated by the person from the Six of Cups. The Two of Swords indicates that this could lead to feelings of confusion, where a choice needs to be made but not knowing which way to jump, creating a deadlock or stalemate situation. The Seven of Swords could present an unexpected twist to matters but also informs Laura that this is the card of speech, talk, and diplomacy so may require the careful handling of the matter.

There is the possibility here, with the information we have from the future grouping, that the Page could link to the Knight of Cups, which in turn could connect to the Five and Seven of Cups in the home area and the potential of the Five of Pentacles in the love area. The inference being that someone from Laura's past could contact her with a romantic proposition and create a personal dilemma. Whilst there is no one else around her at the moment, and we have no male court card in the reading to identify with, I cannot say more, except that it is someone known to her. Clearly the repercussions of such a situation could be damaging to the fragility of her marriage, in happy but early recovery days.

I refer Laura back to the logical thought that will be required, shown by the Justice card in the Anchor, and the warning from the Five of Pentacles at the end of the love area, when she is currently experiencing the Nine of Cups. I explained to Laura that it was not my position to judge, only to pass on what I see, and if I saw wonderful cards connected to this then I would tell her, but my concern was that with the indications we had before us she might misjudge something and end up in a worse situation.

The Key card of the reading showed Laura successfully juggling everything, which again seemed very pertinent to the present: her busy but careful balance of home, work, and the reconciled relationship.

The Anchor
CENTRAL POSITION: THE WORLD
IMMEDIATE FUTURE: TEMPERANCE
WISHES: THE FOOL
THE FUTURE: THE HERMIT

The final cards of the Anchor have not been covered yet, so we move over to this area to see what else we can find here. I tell Laura that the Fool card in her wishes area suggests that what she really wants is a completely new and different start. Laura looked quite surprised and said that was exactly how she felt. Since she had left modelling she wished they could just move away to somewhere where nobody knew them, to start completely fresh and anonymous. She had enjoyed modelling initially and everything had gone extremely well, but when she changed her management company she later realised this had been a mistake, resulting in advice and decisions that had badly impacted both her and her family. On a personal level, she had enjoyed the glamour, the lifestyle, and an amazing boost to her self-confidence, yet she realised it became an unrealistic world, and one where unfortunately she finally saw the downside. With home and careers it wasn't possible to just move abroad and start again. The Hanging Man and the Five of Cups resonate for her here, and she stated that there was so much of her reading to which she could relate.

I pointed out to Laura that she had a wonderful card sitting central to her reading, the World, which shows success and feeling a sense of accomplishment with her attainments. This card is already in her path and where she is aiming for, so it is within her reach and shouldn't be too far away.

With Temperance in the immediate future position I advise Laura that patience and moderation will be required in order to achieve her aims but the harmonious aspect of this gentle card also brings a lovely element of healing into her life. Temperance can also bring reconciliation, which may echo with the Six of Cups from the future grouping in the Life Spread, since she has already reconciled with her husband. Seeing Temperance, I inform Laura that the message from the cards is to take her time and exercise moderation in all areas; now isn't the time to go rushing into anything, particularly due to some of the warning signs that have been covered in various areas. Laura admits that patience is not one of her best virtues.

As if to strengthen the message, the Hermit shows that Laura is heading towards a time where a period of introspection will be required, a time of deep reflection and soul-searching. However, it also informs her that within herself she will already know the answer, she will just need some quiet time to access it. Taken in context with the rest of her reading I told Laura that in the future I felt she would be looking at everything in her life at a very deep level. As Justice is the card that shows the need for a balanced mind, so Temperance is the card for balanced emotions. As we follow the path leading up to the Hermit, there are strong messages here reminding her to try and be logical, balanced, and patient when faced with the deliberations of her future.

Laura said she could relate to a great deal of what had been said in her reading and the cards had reflected what she is feeling, against what is evident from external appearances. (This could be the reason why the cards had seemed contradictory.)

Much of what she had to say about her living situation and her newfound contentment tended to reflect that she was already experiencing the vibrations of the Justice card in her love area. With other indications, and from what she has said, it can be a little worrying that she is taking such a practical and logical approach to her situation. The cards that are lacking here, the element that is missing, are the loving aspects that would indicate her heart is happy. The Ten of Cups for instance, the Two or Three of Cups and similar, are all strangely missing. The Nine of Cups sits in isolation as she tries to hold her wish together, the happiness of the family unit, at least outwardly achieved. The fact that the Cup cards I refer to are not here does not necessarily mean they are not being experienced. I feel the Tarot will provide those cards that are most needed in order to convey their message within the twenty-one cards. These are my thoughts, not shared with Laura.

I don't feel it is my place to offer my personal opinion but to read what I have before me—and in this instance, not to point out what is missing. Laura is trying very hard to apply the practical measures to a reconciled marriage, which is always fragile enough, given that there are past hurts to work through. I feel that at this point she doesn't need me suggesting that emotionally she doesn't appear happy, to influence her thinking or create doubts in her mind. This is a conclusion that the cards would clearly state, or she would.

Meanwhile, as she works through her situation, I consider my position is to provide the guidance as it is shown to me. Should her situation change and she returns for further guidance, we would see how things have progressed and offer the information given in the cards at that time.

There are a few other things to note with this reading. Firstly, you may wonder why the cards are not more conclusive. Why are there only these suggestions running through the reading? My thoughts regarding this are that with the Life Spread, I would expect the cards to be far clearer if the situation were closer in time. From my experience of working with this spread, if events were imminent then the indications would leave us in no doubt. I believe we could be looking at a potential situation that may still be developing. It is dependant upon various actions taking place and therefore the outcome is, as yet, still unknown.

As if to echo some of my thoughts the next reading provided further insight.

Additional Spread: Celtic Cross

Laura felt she would like to try and find out more about the situation that had been shown in her work area. The cards from the Life Spread were collected and handed to Laura for shuffling whilst she asked if there were anything untoward happening in her business of which she needed to be aware.

The cards drawn appeared to have little connection to the question asked; sometimes this can happen if there is a more pressing issue deemed more relevant. The reading seemed to relate more to Laura's personal and love life.

Now we have some cup cards in evidence! The straight line made up of the Three of Cups, the Two of Cups, the Hierophant, and the Lovers with their relevant associations immediately made me think of Laura's marriage. Cups occupy the present, the filter it is working through.

The Page of Wands, which represents good news arriving, possibly in connection to work or of a business orientation, is in the most recent past position. Laura feels this must be when her husband received the news regarding his new job, as this was fairly recent and she cannot otherwise place the card.

The Lovers in her crowning thoughts together with the Two of Pentacles in the hopes and wishes position shows Laura keeping the balance and reflects to us how important this is to her. Also the Sun, the most positive card in the Tarot, appears in her area of apprehensions, so this is most encouraging. It also tells its own story, as often this card teamed together with the basis of the situation in position three provides further insight, as in this case—the Hierophant. We can now see what a mistake it would have been had I shared my earlier thoughts, for here are the very cards I was concerned were missing in the story.

The Knight of Wands can represent a long journey or a change of residence. It is difficult to tell which without the back-up of other cards; although this could also point to the cards that were in the personal area of the Life Spread—the Knight of Cups and the Ten of Pentacles, suggesting property—and therefore could be a move or new family home. As other people are

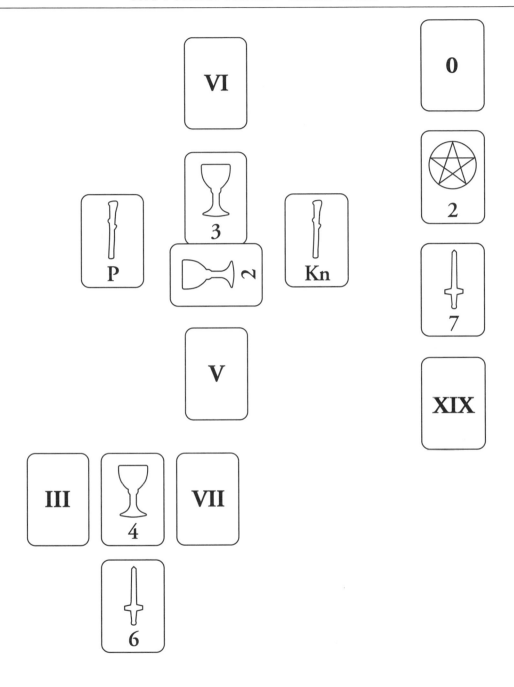

viewing the situation we have the Seven of Swords, which could point to an unexpected twist to events, but also the card of handling something diplomatically.

The Fool as the outcome card points to a new and unexpected situation coming in from out the blue. Since the sixth and the tenth card both refer to the future there should be a connection between the two; it may not be obvious to us at the moment but should be evident in the fullness of time. With the Fool in her wishes position of the Anchor, it may just be that Laura gets her wish of a new start in some way but with the Seven of Swords it may not be in the way she expects.

The cards in the Reader's Fan—the Chariot and the Six of Swords—seem to strengthen the journey suggested by the Knight of Wands. The Empress backs up the marriage cards we have been shown; the Four of Cups echoes some of the thoughts from the previous reading. The job of the Reader's Fan, however, is not usually to extend the reading, only to provide further background information for the reader.

Whatever the situation that appears to be brewing in Laura's work area it cannot be more important than the cards we have been shown, since they are not related to her question concerning this. It would also tend to suggest that it is containable. Laura is very pleased with her reading, mindful of the messages from the first spread, but looking forward to forthcoming events.

Results and Feedback

Within the timeframe, everything tended to happen in close proximity.

Two Months Later

Laura was unexpectedly offered a property abroad from a family member, which she was delighted to buy. Whilst she may not be able to move completely out of the country, as she would like, it provides a haven abroad for the family in an area she loves. (Life Spread, personal area: Queen of Cups, Knight of Cups, Ten of Pentacles.)

Since the timing of this was quite close, I feel that this was probably the situation the Celtic Cross was also referring to—the Knight of Wands and the Fool with the unexpected twist from the Seven of Swords. Laura stated that the offer did literally come out of nowhere and was very unexpected. In this instance perhaps both meanings for the Knight of Wands were relevant, since the property is abroad, so travel and change of residence are both appropriate.

A week later Laura's husband was made redundant from his new post. However, they are hopeful that a specialist recruitment agency will be able to find him an alternative position. (Five of Pentacles at the end of the love area.)

Straight after this Laura had to let some of her staff go. Numerous conduct issues had been brewing, creating a lot of problems for the business, but an incident of theft was discovered, resulting in dismissal. After leaving her employment, Laura found the employees were poaching her clients. This became evident when customers failed to arrive for booked appointments but never rang to cancel. Once she started making some enquiries she also discovered that her former employees had been privately offering services to her customers at least a month prior to their dismissal. Whilst the work area had been accurate so had the sequence of events that the cards provided (the Devil, the High Priestess, Five of Swords).

The mystery of the connection with the Hierophant was perhaps also answered here. Laura told me that she had brought in an experienced businessman whom she knew and respected to advise her. He had witnessed various situations with her employees and ultimately it was he who dealt with their dismissal. As a result, Laura had started a college course in order to improve her professional expertise and qualify in an area she had previously relied upon by those she employed, so as not to leave her so vulnerable in the future. So, whilst the church had been relevant as her landlord, the Hierophant represented the mentor who was connected to the dismissals and also the college, as the educational institution. Whilst I could have listed them further to Laura at the time, there is no way I would have made that connection. It is fascinating to later discover how the cards applied.

Three Months Later

Laura contacted me to say that her husband had found a new position. It still involved constant travel and regular periods away from home but he had also been promoted now.

Referring back to the Life Spread, remember the apparent contradiction of the Five of Pentacles at the end of the love area and the Ten of Pentacles at the end of the personal area? Even if you are not aware of how the interpretation fits it is worth pointing out what you see to the seeker, as once events unfold they can be more appropriate than you realise or could have predicted at the time. I feel it also provides a good example to demonstrate to us how the Five of Pentacles showed an isolated event with no further bad implications; quite literally, due to its lone position of apparent disconnection to the surrounding cards and no further reference or continuation of the theme. When the area cards do not flow together like a sentence in the Life Spread they can show a separate situation.

In the meantime, Laura had hired some new employees that she was happy with, so she felt that life was not only settling back down again but also showing further improvement.

Since her reading, an old friend had emerged on the scene and whilst Laura enjoyed his friendship she realised that it could too easily develop further. She said she had agonised over her decision, as she knew her friend would be upset and she would miss him, but she had explained as kindly as possible that she felt it best if he not contact her anymore. (Future area: Six of Cups, Page of Cups, Two of Swords, Seven of Swords.) Laura certainly seemed to be applying the balanced, logical thought of the Justice card shown in the love area of the Anchor.

Five Months Later

It appeared that the Hierophant connected to Laura's landlord did have a further part to play after all. During the period that the structural repairs were being done to the building and her business was inoperable she did not pay rent for that one month, keeping up all other payments. To her horror she arrived one morning to find the locks on the building changed and notices on the door by her landlord. She sincerely wished she had taken the advice to have her solicitor check the lease, as a clause in her contract allowed them to legally do this, due to the missed payment and regardless of being unable to operate her business. Fortunately, she cleared the matter up with them immediately but was left with an additional bill for lock replacements and some embarrassing publicity to her business.

Six Months Later

Laura informed me that it was interesting how much information had come to light regarding her former employee, which included similar but unreported past problems with previous employers. However, she is really pleased with the way the business partnership has now progressed, as for the first time since setting up they can see tangible results and have finally turned the corner to making it successful. With the new team in place she states that the workplace has a more pleasant atmosphere and life is calmer as a result. Looking back she says she can't believe how stressful it was previously but the experience has left her far wiser. With these final words it appears Laura's reading has fully played out.

In Laura's Own Words

I had been to Josie for readings in the past and was astonished by their accuracy, so I was really looking forward to seeing what she had to tell me. I had a lot of problems at home and I was looking for guidance or some sort of answers that would help and guide me.

When I went home I thought about what had been said; my cards had always been right before but I wasn't quite prepared for the accuracy of this reading! Certain things happened at home and at work and they were exactly what Josie told me to watch for. She had warned me to watch out for someone at my workplace that I may not be able to trust, it was only shortly afterwards I found out an employee was stealing from me. I knew straightaway that's what the cards were warning me of, so in a way I was kind of prepared for this happening and it certainly made me double check the till on a night. When the incident actually happened I remember thinking about it and I could hear Josie's words ringing in my head!

With everything that has happened I feel that the readings helped me through the past few months. I have been more careful and there were things I never would have thought to check, otherwise it could have been a lot worse than the way it turned out.

Reader's Tips
Various Interpretations of a Card and Linking Themes

Laura's reading offers an excellent example as to how various interpretations and aspects of a card can apply in different ways. For instance, the Hierophant in the work area of the Anchor was relevant as the helpful mentor that Laura turned to and was instrumental in solving the situation brewing in her work area of the Life Spread, her return to college as a result of this experience and, finally, the situation that occurred with the church as her landlord.

Aside from interpreting the card area groups we can note how each clue provides its own story and how that contributes towards the final interpretation. In this instance: the apparent contradictions, even the "leap-frog" effect of the separate cards across four areas of Laura's Life Spread that seemed to link together. In the end, all held a story within the story, for isn't that so often a reflection of our lives? For me it was a reminder of the value of pointing these factors out to the seeker. Sometimes it makes perfect sense to them at the time and provides relevant information; at other times it seems to make little sense to either of us … until everything slots into place with the results afterwards.

Part of the agreement with the participants in the book was that they would feedback the events as they happened, so we have the benefit of recording them and tracking the results to see how the cards applied to their various situations. I am sure other Tarot readers will also tell you that sometimes people are excited and call you up just to let you know what happened; sometimes they return and become regular visitors over the years, yet others you may never hear from again, but this does not necessarily mean that your reading wasn't accurate in some way.

Once the seeker has left us our role is complete. We may never know the outcome, but we hope that we did our best in providing a reading that was insightful, empowering, and as helpful as possible in the situations and choices they will face.

The Sceptic

Because it is a situation readers can sometimes find themselves faced with, I wanted to show a reading with someone who was sceptical. Sarah was recommended by a friend and put us in contact with one another. I explained my reason for the book was to help Tarot students and the reading was not to "prove" that Tarot works, so all I asked was that she be open-minded. Sarah agreed and the date was set.

Sarah had never had a Tarot reading before and admitted she had never even looked at a Tarot deck, so the images were completely unfamiliar to her. She informed me her experience "of those kinds of things" related to people found on holiday seafronts, all claiming to be authentic Romany gypsies, who try and hassle her into having a reading or buying a charm lest she suffer bad luck. Sarah recounts how she was once invited to attend someone's home with a group of friends for a visiting psychic; she had felt disappointed, as nothing said had related to her or her friends. Needless to say, her experiences to date had not been very positive.

Given Sarah's previous experiences, and since she had never had a Tarot reading before, I was even more careful to explain the procedure we would be following. Before we began I knew that Sarah was in her forties, divorced with two children, and works in the medical profession.

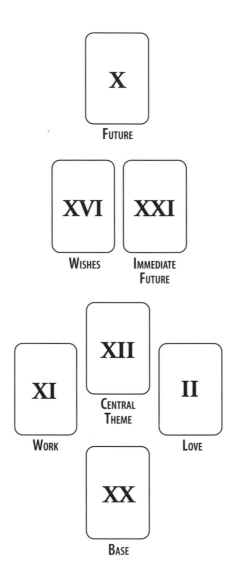

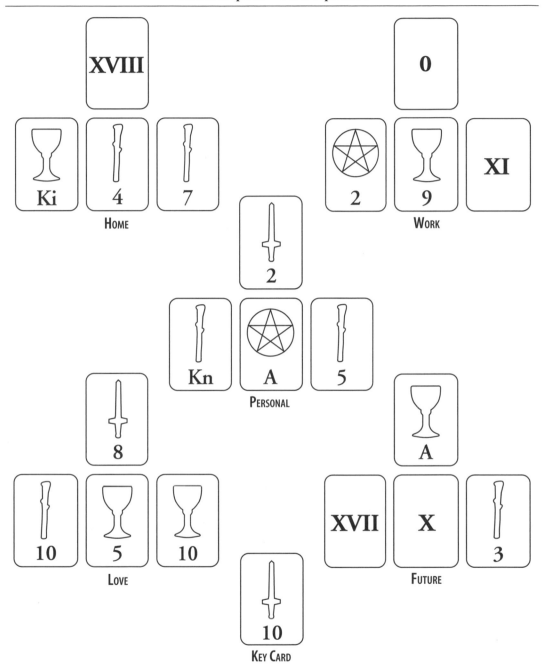

First Impressions

Whilst laying out the cards I am looking for synergies in the spreads, repeat messages that appear to back one another up, or linking themes.

- The Justice card repeated in both work areas of each spread.
- The Wheel of Fortune repeated in both future areas of each spread.
- The Hanging Man central to the Anchor with the Two of Swords as the first card of the Life Spread.
- The Tower in the hopes and wishes section of the Anchor and the Ten of Swords as the Key card of the Life Spread. Also the Judgement card in the first position of the Anchor.
- The Ten of Cups in the love area and Ace of Cups in the future area of the Life Spread.
- Three Tens in close proximity of the Life Spread—transitional phase of completion.

Since there are only a few brief moments before starting to interpret the reading to the seeker let me just relay to you the links I was following in my mind. Similar to Simon's reading from chapter 2, we have the Tower sitting in the hopes and wishes section of the Anchor, usually reflecting a strong desire for change. Together with the Ten of Swords as the Key card, the Eight of Swords and Five of Cups in the love area of the Life Spread, I am already drawn to what lies here and suspect there is a recent breakup. The Hanging Man central to the Anchor may represent feeling life in suspension, which corresponds to the Two of Swords as the first card dealt in the personal area, showing a stalemate situation. We also have the Moon in the home area.

However, these are my initial impressions so I feel it is always safer to work through the reading. For me to fully consider these connections longer and look deeper into the rest of the spread would leave an uncomfortable silence, and this tends to make people nervous or tense because they immediately think something is wrong. Usually I find it better to mentally note things and move on, rather than dive in and potentially get it wrong—or shock the seeker if it's right, which would hardly show sensitivity to their situation. Whatever I'm looking at, or may have to prepare her for, a calm environment is more conducive to a successful reading for her and less stress for me!

The Anchor
BASE POSITION: JUDGEMENT

In the present position of the Anchor, Judgement can represent renewal and revival. I explained to Sarah it can symbolise standing at a crossroads of life in readiness for a new beginning. Having cleared away old debris and learnt lessons from the past, there is a sense of feeling ready to move forward again, wiser from past experience. Since it can show revival and resurrection, Judgement can also bring something from the past back into play, such as reconciliation. I asked Sarah if she felt any of this connected to her circumstances at the moment and she said she could relate to some of it, although from her response I didn't feel as if we were hitting the right spot yet, so to speak.

The Anchor
LOVE AREA: THE HIGH PRIESTESS

I didn't feel the High Priestess in the love area was going to be particularly helpful at this point. The difficulty with this card is that telling people that a secret may soon become known to them and be to their benefit, yet not be able to tell them *what* it is, can be awkward! I have found that the High Priestess doesn't give up her mysteries easily. Trying to open this card further in a Celtic Cross reading, for instance, rarely provides an answer and often sends me round in a circle. Whilst providing the meaning of the card to Sarah I didn't dwell on it here as I thought there were other areas of the reading that could be more helpful at this point. However, Sarah leapt in to tell me she had gone through a breakup recently and said she wouldn't be surprised if there weren't more information to come out. She then asked if I would like her to tell me more about it but I said I would prefer to go over other areas of the reading with her first, to explain what I could see relating to it, and then she could expand further and we could discuss it in just a moment, if she didn't mind. Sarah agreed.

The Anchor
CENTRAL POSITION: THE HANGING MAN
HOPES AND WISHES: THE TOWER
The Life Spread
PERSONAL AREA: TWO OF SWORDS

The central card of the Anchor is usually an important placement because all the other cards surround it, often making it the heart of the reading. The Hanging Man can show a feeling of life being in suspension and made the link here with the first card of the Life Spread, the Two of Swords, which can also show a feeling of deadlock or stalemate.

Sarah agreed this felt right, so I moved on to the Tower in the hopes and wishes section of the Anchor, explaining that normally when this card appeared in this position, people feel as if they want a bit of a shake-up in their life, even to the extent of radical change. Sarah confirmed this, leaning forward inquisitively to investigate the cards on the table before us and commented on how beautiful the pictures were. I felt relieved that we had found our first area where things appeared to be slotting into place for her and starting to make sense. Between Judgement, the Hanging Man, the Tower, and the Two of Swords, it felt as if we had made our first proper link.

Moving back to the Hanging Man, I explained that whilst it can indicate life being in a period of suspension, it also carries a message of looking at situations from a different perspective in order to gain a better understanding. This "think outside the box" card suggests that solutions can be found by looking at things from a slightly different stance. It can also represent making a small sacrifice now in order to gain something of greater benefit in the longer term. I also explained that she had some pretty good cards that showed some positive events to come, which we would cover shortly.

The Life Spread
Work Area: The Fool, Two of Pentacles, Nine of Cups, Justice
The Anchor
Work Area: Justice

Justice in the work area was most interesting, as it is repeated in both spreads. I explained that Justice symbolised taking a logical approach to matters but could also represent documents or agreements with legal significance. Sarah told me that she cannot think of anything that applies here at work at the moment. However, because Justice is also sitting at the end of the Life Spread work area, I feel this might still be to come.

The Fool and Nine of Cups looked rather exciting with the potential for something new to come in unexpectedly, together with contracts from Justice. With the Two of Pentacles to the far left, this position often reveals the past or present in the particular area it represents. The Two shows confidently juggling more than one project and when I relayed this to Sarah she told me she had a secondary evening job to supplement her full-time day work. As a lone parent she was used to working long hours to support herself and family.

When I asked if anything new had presented itself recently she told me that it hadn't and was unlikely to, as she had gone as high as she could in her own position. Together with the Nine of Cups (the "wish card"), she definitely felt it could not be in her current place of work or career. Sarah informed me that so far as a wish in her work is concerned she would love to do voluntary work in a third-world country for six months. However, she didn't feel it was applicable because it was something she could do when she chose, and unfortunately the timing really wasn't right for her at the moment due to family commitments.

With this considered, I asked her to stay alert, as with the Fool the new opportunity could present itself unexpectedly, although the idea should excite her. Justice could represent contracts and agreements relating to it, although it could be that she will be looking at the situation in a logical way when it arose.

The Life Spread
PERSONAL AREA: TWO OF SWORDS, KNIGHT OF WANDS, ACE OF PENTACLES, FIVE OF WANDS

Aside from the Two of Swords, we had difficulty relating the other cards to any present circumstances in Sarah's life at the moment, indicating they are still to follow.

The Knight of Wands usually signifies a change of residence or a long journey. The Ace of Pentacles can represent lump sums of money, gifts, or important documents relating to material concerns. Quite often these two together tend to show when someone is buying or selling property or moving, due to the amount of money involved and the house deeds (if buying) or tenancy agreements (if renting). This would normally be my first choice. Sarah informed me that she was very settled where she lives, it suited her in many ways and so moving was not something she had any thoughts towards.

If the Knight of Wands indicates travel it is usually long distance, such as travelling abroad; the Ace of Pentacles could represent travel documents and currency. Sarah had hoped to go abroad but plans hadn't materialised, in fact she laughed that she had let her passport lapse. With the Five of Wands sitting on the end, suggesting all kinds of petty obstacles, we thought it might be a good idea to get it renewed, just in case.

I explained that the Five of Wands could be wearisome but, as stated, the obstacles or conflicts that the card represents are of a minor nature, they will be evident but not insurmountable. As there appeared to be no further indications in the spread suggesting moving or travel I informed Sarah that she would need to remain open here since I could not advise further.

The Life Spread
HOME AREA: THE MOON, KING OF CUPS,
FOUR OF WANDS, SEVEN OF WANDS

The Moon, as the Key card in the home area, can show emotions swinging back and forth but can also suggest deception, and before I could expand on the rest of the meaning Sarah interrupted to say that this hit the nail right on the head. She went on to say that this was the very reason she had split up with her partner. As the King of Cups was in the first position I told her I would provide a description of the type of person represented by this card to see if she recognised him. The King of Cups is usually noted by his easygoing and friendly nature, liked by most and seldom with enemies, they can be creative and caring which may show in their choice of profession. Sarah seemed quite surprised by this, "That's him!" she exclaimed, "That exactly describes my ex."

The interesting thing in this for me was twofold: being followed by the Four of Wands shows stability, a feeling of being satisfied with what has already been accomplished—and sometimes holidays, a time of rest and relaxation with those you love. Secondly, if you look at the love area, the Five of Cups moves straight to the Ten of Cups. My point here is that in both placements there is no actual split shown, as such.

We move straight from one situation to the next, although I will cover this more fully in the love area cards. At this stage I was still treading cautiously with my thoughts. Things were going well for Sarah's reading so far and I didn't want to race ahead and get it wrong or make her pull back, as by now she was fully involved and enjoying her reading.

I explained that although her partner had gone her home situation appeared to be stable, or had stabilised quickly. His disappearance didn't seem to have upset the balance at home, although this did seem at odds with the emotional push-pull being felt by the Moon. Sarah pointed out that he hadn't been living with her full-time although he had spent the majority of his time with her, so she thought her home was stable and otherwise unaffected by his departure.

The Seven of Wands represents someone confidently, and figuratively speaking, defending their corner, in terms of their ideals and beliefs. It is the card of being true to yourself and not being afraid to stand your ground if required, regarding your integrity and deeply felt values. Sarah said she felt this card very accurately described her personality and in the situation with her ex, it had been due to her zero tolerance policy on lies that had led to the split. At this point, the card seemed to stand alone since it was in the future position. (I came back to it later, as you will see further into the reading.)

The Life Spread
RELATIONSHIP AREA: EIGHT OF SWORDS, TEN OF WANDS,
FIVE OF CUPS, TEN OF CUPS
KEY CARD: TEN OF SWORDS

By now Sarah had revealed a number of things regarding her breakup but we hadn't discussed it in depth. The Eight of Swords as the Key card shows feelings of restriction and "mental monsters" can be preventing forward movement. In the image the woman is bound and blindfold, preventing her from moving out of the circle of swords that surround her, but also from seeing the clarity that the swords contain—the double-edged aspect often found in the suit of Swords (please forgive the pun!).

The Ten of Wands represents feeling overwhelmed or overburdened by a situation and this is followed by the Five of Cups showing a sense of loss and regrets, sometimes a feeling of betrayal. However, I pointed out that I couldn't see anyone else involved from the cards, so it didn't appear to be a betrayal of that nature. I moved straight to the Ten of Swords here, the Key card, representing disappointment and loss. At this stage Sarah reported that there hadn't been anyone else involved but the cards very accurately described her feelings and she had felt enormously disappointed by his behaviour.

As you can probably see, I took my time approaching the Ten of Cups. I have previously been faced with people who were still emotionally upset over a breakup, and when confronted by a lovely card such as this, they became quite defensive and argumentative. If I have fairly significant cards, I like to gauge the person's reaction before I release the message to them—otherwise it is quite often a case of shooting the messenger! Being sensitive to the seeker's mindset and approaching the subject accordingly makes life easier for both of us. As readers we know what this card represents, but whether the seeker is ready to hear it can be another matter.

I think my biggest lesson with this kind of situation came as a result of a reading for a lady who was divorced; in her Celtic Cross, her ex-husband's card lead directly to the Ten of Cups. In that instance there were other indications to back this up in the other positions, but when I relayed the information to her, she was absolutely adamant they would never get back together, let alone be in a committed relationship again—*certainly* not marriage. She was horrified and argued her case. I smiled and explained that I was only relaying the message the cards gave me; that this was the interpretation of them, and whatever came up and what she chose to do was her own decision. I heard they remarried within the year.

Through experiences like this, you begin to trust your cards. Regardless of what you think, or however unlikely it may seem to the seeker based on what they have told you, it is best to stay true to the meanings you have attached to the cards, rather than trying to make them fit the situation as it appears to them at the time. However, this can be easier said than done once the logical mind steps in. I tend to think of what comedians say about the punch line of a joke—delivery and timing are everything. An odd analogy, perhaps, since a proportion of the time we are not always delivering a message the seeker wants to hear.

The difference in this situation with Sarah's cards is that we have no other marriage indicators. The Ten of Cups alone may bring contentment and happiness in the heart department but at this stage at least, it does not appear to lead any further. It may be that this is a possibility that reaches further out on the radar of time than we can pick up at the moment.

I explained to Sarah that the cards here looked very interesting (a word I use a lot in readings; as you will see, it gets me through all kinds of situations!). Whilst I could appreciate how she felt and heard what she had said, the Ten of Cups with its message of a happy and contented relationship appeared to be a most unlikely card to be sitting right alongside the Five. However, what I found most intriguing about it was the fact that we went straight to the Ten from the Five. I felt that this either meant the relationship would follow the literal interpretation of moving from the Five situation to the Ten with the relationship the Five was referring to—or that an amazingly good relationship was going to land as if from nowhere. I explained that my reason for this was due to the placement of the cards, as there was nothing in between them to show a new relationship entering. It was possible, since we do have an Ace of Cups in the final section of the Life Spread, but given what we have there was also a strong possibility that it could refer to her ex-partner. Sarah was quite amazed and didn't bite my head off—a bonus.

Sarah explained that it had been a wonderful relationship but she had felt so disappointed when she discovered a string of lies. When I questioned her over the nature of them she stated that the ridiculous part was that they were so trivial and meaningless, they weren't malicious or used to cover up bad behaviour. Our discussion on this deepened as Sarah expressed her inner conflict (Eight of Swords) about the situation. Here we had a wonderful relationship, in every way except for some meaningless storytelling, but they were not used to intentionally mislead, betray, or hurt her and appeared to have no function at all. Her partner was younger than her, one of the reasons she had resisted the relationship before allowing herself to finally become involved. She had felt there was a possibility that, although mature for his age, her partner felt the need to try to be "more than he was" in the eyes of older company.

At this stage I handed her the Five of Cups, asking her to look at the image in the card and to look at the cups in the card. I asked her to describe what she saw and she covered the man grieving over the three spilt cups with two cups standing upright behind him. I explained how literal the message of the card could be. The man was focussed upon what was lost in the situation but the two cups standing upright represented there were still good things to be found, he just couldn't see them at the present time. Quite often the Five represents that something good still remains. With different cards it would qualify different interpretations, but here this was not the case.

Sarah further explained that she just couldn't tolerate any kind of lying due to the circumstances of her first marriage and the behaviour of her ex-husband, which had included a string of affairs and violence. As she opened up and verbalised it, she had a moment of personal insight, as she realised that her partner's behaviour had made an association with that of her ex-husband, which immediately triggered an old response in her reaction.

It seemed an appropriate moment to go through some of the cards' messages due to their particular placements and a relevant connection contained in them.

The Anchor
LOVE AREA: THE HIGH PRIESTESS
CENTRAL POSITION: THE HANGING MAN
The Life Spread
HOME AREA: THE MOON

The High Priestess reveals secrets that are soon to become known that will be to her benefit in the love area. The Hanging Man, which is so central to the reading, suggests looking at a situation another way and taking a different approach, in order to gain a better perspective and gain something better in the longer term. The Moon also has an illusionary quality, like moonlight in the darkness creating shadows that are not what they seem once the lights are switched on. With the Moon it is always better to reserve judgement until all the facts become known, as at the moment they are lurking under the surface and not fully revealed.

I informed Sarah that the cards suggest there was more to yet come out in the situation and if she could be open-minded and take the message of the Hanging Man on board then perhaps she would be looking at a different result, of course this would remain her choice. If the Ten of Cups did not refer to her most recent relationship then perhaps the Five had led her

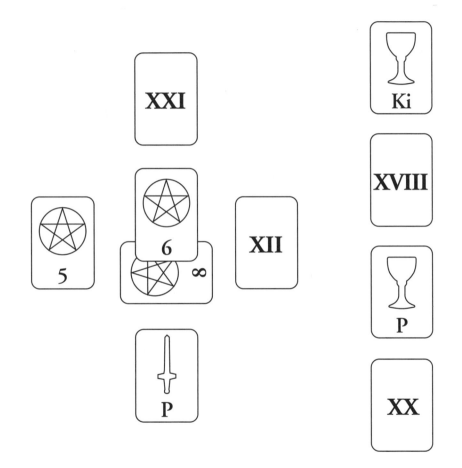

to a place of greater understanding that would assist her old behaviour patterns if the Ten did bring a different relationship instead. Sarah was fascinated as she could see how this applied.

The Life Spread
FUTURE OUTCOME: ACE OF CUPS, THE STAR,
WHEEL OF FORTUNE, THREE OF WANDS
The Anchor
IMMEDIATE AND FUTURE OUTCOME: THE WORLD AND
THE WHEEL OF FORTUNE

The Ace of Cups, representing the beginning of love and happiness, can bring a new relationship. It can sometimes represent renewal and we do have the Star (healing) here. However, this is not an interpretation I tend to use with this card, usually relying on Judgement, Temperance, and the Six of Cups for revivals. This Ace can bring the start of something new that brings emotional fulfilment. The Star as a card of faith, hope, and healing assures of more promising and better times ahead. The Wheel continues this theme as it opens up a whole new chapter beginning and is positively aspected by surrounding cards. The Three of Wands shows initial success and progression of plans, this can often be connected to work related matters, although not always.

The final cards in the Anchor are in tune with the final area of the Life Spread. With the World in the immediate future of the Anchor there is a sense of successful conclusion. The Wheel repeated as Sarah's final card re-emphasises that a new cycle is due to commence and it will be of a positive nature due to the surrounding cards. Once she moves beyond the position of the Hanging Man these wonderful final cards provide an uplifting message that life is due to improve for Sarah in the future.

Having covered all the cards in both spreads, I asked Sarah if there was anything further she wanted clarified, or wanted to ask about that had not shown in the reading. Sarah said she would really like to know more about the realtionship situation from the spread, to see if it was her ex or someone new.

Additional Spread: Celtic Cross

The cards from the Life Spread were gathered and the deck handed back to Sarah. I explained that she would need to shuffle and cut the cards again, as she had before, except this time she needed to focus on a question. Since an "either/or" question could leave us with an ambiguous answer the suggestion was to ask, "What is coming up in my love life?" as then the cards could possibly show us if it was a new or revived relationship. I asked Sarah to focus upon her question and not to stop shuffling too soon, in order for her to make a good link with the cards.

The Six of Pentacles in the present position can show gifts, generosity, and sharing or an increase in finance, crossed by the Eight of Pentacles, which usually represents new work of some description. The Page of Swords can signify disappointing news or delays and often may reveal more information about the background, so could in some way be connected to the Six of Pentacles. It didn't seem to make a great deal of sense to me so I asked Sarah if she could provide any link between these cards. She looked rather surprised and said her ex had bought her a piece of jewellery as a gift but she hadn't received it because they had fallen out in the meantime, and she had met him through the new second job she had taken. Whilst it hadn't made a great deal of sense to me it had for Sarah, so the starting position was quite accurate.

The Five of Pentacles shows the most recent past and is a card of loss, although in this instance it was the emotional loss. Sarah's crowning thoughts and hopes and fears (cards 5 and 9) show the push-pull conflict she is currently experiencing, vying between the two cards. The World is what she's hoping for but the Moon is upsetting her balance as her emotions swing back and forth. Sarah said this was just how she felt because it had been such a good relationship.

The Hanging Man makes another appearance in the immediate future and so will in some way relate to the outcome card, since both cards deal with the future. The outcome card is the King of Cups, who we have already established as the one representing her ex. A court card in the final position informs us that the answer is associated with whoever this card may be, so the end result will depend upon the actions or behaviour of her partner.

Looking at the Anchor we can now see why the Hanging Man is central and pivotal to the reading because we have further information to show that it plays a big part in the immediate future and ultimately leads to the King. Sarah's reassessment of the matter by looking at things from a different perspective is also a key component here. As this card appears to play such an important role I handed it to Sarah for her to examine, as before with the Five of Cups.

In the apprehensions area, Judgement, as the card of revival, also makes another appearance. It was at this point that Sarah told me that her ex had already been in contact with her asking if they could get back together. I smiled and pointed to the Judgement card in the Anchor and reminded her that this had been our starting position in the first reading. (It would have been helpful if I had known this back then!)

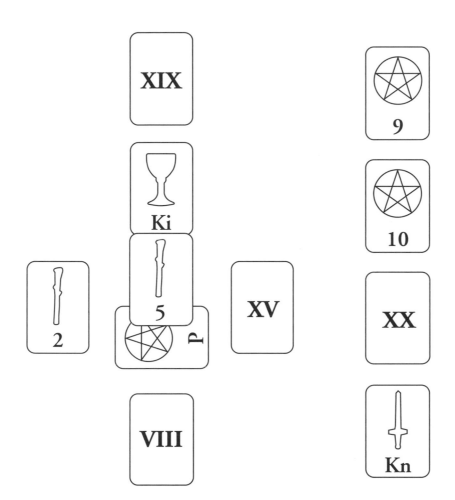

As other people are looking at the situation the Page of Cups represents messages, usually of a happy nature that affect us emotionally, so my feeling was that she would be hearing from him again.

Since her ex-partner's card had appeared in the last position, I told Sarah we could take his card and move the reading further, if she wished. This time, however, I asked Sarah to concentrate on him and to focus upon asking for the reading to continue from this card. Needless to say, she was keen to do so!

Additional Spread: Celtic Cross 2

Although we have taken the King of Cups as representing Sarah's ex, the spread is still read as hers, not his. The Five of Wands as the first card dealt now provides more information about what is covering the situation with the King of Cups. As recalled from previously, in shorthand the Five of Wands represents petty obstacles and challenges. The filter card, the atmosphere if you will, that the Five is working through shows messages coming in that could bring welcome change.

At the base of the situation, Strength is a good card to have, not only representing the more feminine qualities of diplomacy and patience, but it can also be quite a potent card for a woman, providing a certain magnetism to male energy.

In the most recent past of the situation the Two of Wands finds form, having moved beyond the creative expression, ideas, and energy found in the Ace, now looking to the future and the choices these will bring.

The Sun as the crowning card is far better balanced here against the Ten of Pentacles in the ninth position of hopes and wishes. Remembering that we have moved forward slightly in time (this is a continuation reading) we can see that Sarah's thoughts on the potential of the situation have improved. Since the Sun is from the major arcana and the Ten of Pentacles from the minors, the indication is that she will most likely lean towards the major card. However, these two also read together well as a pair, complementing one another.

The Devil is surrounded by positive cards, so whilst it may still indicate a block in the situation, we can also look to the brighter side of this card, which can also suggest an improvement in her love life—the Devil can be quite a passionate, steamy card in the right circumstances. Big smile from Sarah!

I explained to Sarah that the apprehensions position quite often throws people if they find they have a positive card; oftentimes people want something but also can't quite bring themselves to believe it could happen. The Knight of Swords usually brings a fast-paced energy into play; the speed of events can make them feel almost chaotic because everything happens so quickly. With this card I felt we would be looking at a very short timeframe.

Because Sarah has specifically focussed her attention on her ex-partner, the eighth position shows how he is or will be viewing the situation. Here again we have the Judgement card, so his desire to reconcile and resurrect the relationship is still showing strongly.

In the final position, the Nine of Pentacles may seem puzzling on first inspection; sometimes this card can be interpreted as solitary pleasure, but it does not necessarily mean the person may be alone or without relationship. Independent, self-sufficient, or detached people can show this card, representing feeling secure within themselves and their accomplishments. With the Devil leading to the Nine of Pentacles, this does not seem to be providing us with a committed future either. If we consider Sarah's relationship background and the fact that she has successfully raised two children through her own work and efforts as a lone parent, it is unlikely she would want to lose this sense of independence. Sarah confirmed that she wanted to enjoy having a relationship but certainly needed to feel her own independence within it, and was pleased with this outcome card.

The indications from all the readings suggest the potentiality exists for reconciliation in the relationship but from the first Celtic Cross the result will in some way rely upon her partner's actions. With the Hanging Man as the central card of the Anchor and in the sixth position of the first Celtic Cross, it also relies upon Sarah's viewpoint on the matter in the future and it can suggest making some sacrifices. Can she work through her existing perceptions? What will she decide to do?

Results and Feedback

After the reading, Sarah said she was completely amazed by the information the cards had provided and the depth they went into. She had thoroughly enjoyed our session and felt she had learned a great deal about herself, things she inwardly knew but had never really given great consideration. The reading had given her the opportunity to see how some of her old behaviour patterns affected her responses and reactions to her current situation.

Two Days Later

I received a phone call from an excited Sarah two days later. "You're not going to believe this," she said, "but I bumped into my ex the very next day and he asked if we could talk things over."

Sarah had agreed. She told me that the High Priestess in the love area had been accurate and they had spent hours just talking about everything that had happened, with much revealed from both sides. "And that Devil card was right on the money! He stayed the night." Enough said!

Sarah said the messages from the cards had helped her deal with the situation and her own feelings much more positively and although she hadn't agreed to a reconciliation just yet, it was now a consideration. She also told me that her reading had completely changed her view about Tarot so she had bought the *Easy Tarot* kit to learn about the cards for herself. A convert! As agreed, she told me she would call when other aspects of her reading manifested.

Two Months Later

Sarah called to say that she wasn't taking things any further with her ex. Although she had heard from him frequently and he wanted them to get back together, she was aware his story-telling behaviour still remained, and so she felt unable to move forward with the relationship. She had analysed everything and felt it wasn't right for her.

Six Months Later

It was some time later that I caught up with Sarah again and heard of her progress. In the course of the conversation there were a couple of incidents that came to light from her reading.

Nothing had happened regarding a move at home or connected to travel. I looked back at the chart from her original reading. The Knight of Wands, Ace of Pentacles, and Five of Wands appeared to remain an unfinished aspect of the reading. It isn't very often that nothing from the cards comes through or applies in some way; usually it is where I have misinterpreted them or the seeker decides on a completely different course of action, thus altering events. At first glance I am at a loss as to what I may have missed. As Sarah is not pursuing the relationship I am quietly wondering if perhaps they would have been connected to this in some way. Then I realise there was a further interpretation to the Knight of Wands I had not applied in Sarah's reading.

With no plans to travel and none to move I ask if she has possibly done any house renovations recently or has plans to do so. Sarah is surprised by this and tells me she has just remodelled half her home. When I asked if there had been expenses and delays she went on to tell me she had ordered and paid for some large pieces of furniture at the time work started but rather inconveniently they seemed fated with problems, with no delivery and long overdue. Sarah informed me that work had started about four months after her reading. Although at the time she had no plans to alter her home, it was a spur of the moment decision and one she was pleased with, or would be once the furniture arrived to complete the job!

The property alteration and renovation aspect of the Knight of Wands is one I never used to make with this card; it came from my friend and Tarot buddy Sheila. Since she had mentioned it a time or two in my own readings with good result it became a later addition to my own interpretations. In Sarah's case I had not mentioned it at all. (I kicked myself—after all I have said about covering the different aspects of a card's various meanings!) However, I am not so sure I would have made the association in the way events turned out though. We were both suitably amazed.

When asked about the wish card in her work area, Sarah reported that her main place of work had become involved with a charity where certain unused or unopened drugs were donated and shipped to third-world countries where they are urgently needed. So whilst she may not be able to travel to Africa just yet, a way of providing assistance found her. Since it deals with prescribed medications, official documentation is connected to it. Sarah also tells me that in her role she is constantly surrounded by, and responsible for, relevant legal documentation. This would have connected with Justice in the work area from the Anchor and provided the link to the Nine of Cups to her main work, an area she felt unlikely her "wish" would manifest. In actuality it did, though not in a way she had anticipated.

There are a couple of points here that I should have realised at the time of Sarah's reading, perhaps more so once her reading progressed with the Celtic Cross. Reading what I had written at the time you may have noticed this yourself. Starting with the Fool, Sarah said that nothing new had presented itself at work and felt it was unlikely. I immediately connected the Fool with the Nine of Cups, yet missed the natural progression of the cards.

Sarah had associated the Two of Pentacles in the Life Spread as relating to the part-time work she had taken on, and once I did her Celtic Cross she said the Eight of Pentacles was her "new" secondary job. The fault here was mine. For once the Two of Pentacles was identified, and since the Fool preceded it, I should have gone back to the Fool and asked if the secondary job was new to her. Asking Sarah about this now she tells me that she had started her second job a few months prior to the reading. However, I could have picked this up when she made reference to the new job in the Celtic Cross reading that followed. Sometimes things seem obvious in retrospect!

This left the Ten of Cups and the future area of the Life Spread as the final question mark.

Eight Months Later

In the final stage of trying to finalise some of the readings I called Sarah to find out if there had been any further developments relating to her love life. Since she had not met anyone new I wondered if the Ten of Cups had been connected to her brief reunion with her ex, although this would still leave the Ace of Cups in mid-air, so even if it had I would have expected the potential of a new relationship to have shown by now. Whilst some parts of a reading can take longer to manifest, everything else in Sarah's reading appeared to be accounted for, so I could only conclude that I must have somehow read this incorrectly. Rather sheepishly Sarah apologised and told me that actually, she had met someone new who was really nice but didn't like to say anything because the situation was still developing. I asked when she had met the new man in her life and she reported that he had arrived on the scene just three weeks after the situation with her ex and, as suggested, landed as if from out of nowhere. I guess that cleared that one up then!

In Sarah's Own Words

At first when Josie laid the cards down I thought to myself, "What am I doing? Cards can't tell you anything!" And that's honestly how I felt. As we started the reading and Josie began to explain the cards, what they meant, and how they could relate to areas in your life, etc., I could see things coming together. I was absolutely amazed and mesmerised by it all. I found the whole experience fascinating, compelling, and an eye-opener. After it was finished I had an uplifted feeling inside, it was fantastic. Since the reading I have bought the book, studied, and am still studying the cards. I'm converted, which I never thought I would be! I would recommend it to anyone, believer or not!

Reader's Tips
Sharing the Cards

One of Sarah's comments was how the images and meanings from the Five of Cups and the Hanging Man had stayed with her after the reading, months later these are still prominent in her mind.

By handing the card to the seeker, having them describe what they see and explaining the meaning of the card you are engaging them in the reading—and also the earlier mentioned learning technique. This works particularly well if you want to emphasise any specific cards from the reading that may seem relevant. If someone is going through a difficult time then sharing an uplifting card that appeared in the reading, such as the Star, provides a positive message that will stay with them afterwards.

Sometimes we forget that as the seeker is sitting opposite us the cards appear upside down to them. This is a pity, since they cannot enjoy the impact of the cards as we do.

Involvement and Icebreaker

On occasion I have sat the seeker in my place, pointing out the cards and talking them through various aspects of their reading. This can be useful at the *end* of the reading, but I found that if I did this at the beginning they are so enchanted with the images I can't get a word in edgeways! This is great for seeker involvement, and seeing which cards leap out and resonate with them is always interesting; it can also be a good icebreaker for people who are tense. However, when you are trying to concentrate on the actual reading it's better that they stay on the other side of the table to begin with. Using the Gilded Tarot always provokes positive responses, as people love the images, so they are very user friendly.

Removing Barriers of the "Big Three"

You can also help to alleviate people's fears if one of the "big three"—the Devil, Death, or the Tower—appears in their reading. These cards are traditionally the most feared yet least understood, and many people will comment in a fearful way if they see any of them. Try placing the card in front of them and talking about it. Invite their feedback and inform them of the card's better aspects. It can be extremely helpful in removing barriers or common misconceptions about Tarot. If you do this, just remember to provide them with one of the more pleasant cards afterwards, as otherwise the image provided may be the one they mainly take away from the reading!

As you can see, I enjoy using an interactive approach. If you are unsure perhaps try inviting the person you're reading for to sit in your place once you have finished the reading and see what you think. I have found the atmosphere completely changes and some people become quite excited as they jump from card to card, touching them, asking questions and commenting on their beauty. Everyone has a favourite and explaining the cards to people in this way is fun too. Why not give it a whirl?

6

The Email Reading ...
with a Twist!

Due to the way I work, I prefer appointments with the seeker in attendance. Everything feels more personal and I enjoy the interaction, often establishing an ongoing working relationship that may last for years. However, with the Internet now providing the ability to connect easily with people all over the world, and by request from members of my site from all kinds of far-flung destinations, I started to provide email readings some years ago.

The email reading that is provided here is a little unusual, as you will hopefully see once we reach the conclusion and where I will provide more information about it. This reading was performed more than a year ago now and has been reproduced here by kind permission of the seeker. In this instance I had her name, date of birth, location, and photograph on her private page on my website; she provided the question but nothing further. The question was, "Will I meet my soul mate?" for a Celtic Cross, as it focuses upon only one question.

For privacy reasons and various Internet-related problems that can occur, all correspondence and readings are posted back to the site. I immediately wrote back to Pauline to let her know I had received payment, but having seen her question asked if she would be kind enough to provide some background information. Her question was a bit broad and I needed to know how to apply the cards' meanings to her personal situation. The site automatically triggers an email to inform someone that a message is waiting, but this is reliant upon them checking their email regularly, or that it gets there in the first place! Unfortunately, a lot of people don't recheck their private area on the site and time was marching on.

With the deadline upon me, and no word back from Pauline, I realised I was going to have to work blind on this one. The cards drawn are provided with the text that was sent back to Pauline. The background to the situation is provided later.

Hi Pauline,

Thank you for entrusting me with your reading, which I hope will be useful to you.

For legal reasons I must inform you that readings must now be classed as "for entertainment purposes only."

This was a very interesting spread particularly since you provided me with no background information and, as I didn't receive a reply back from my request, I was initially concerned that this reading may have been rather patchy.

The most intriguing part of this is with regards to the present time…these cards tend to show that you should already have received a message of an emotional nature, as this is the first card and covers the situation around you in relation to the question. (If you have my book you may wish to look at the section on the Celtic Cross for your interest.)

This card is crossed by the Knight of Cups, which almost always brings offers and invitations of love. So if someone hasn't already asked you it certainly seems to be in the offing.

Another possibility here is that you may have attended a family or group celebration recently (as we have the Three of Cups in the past position) so these three together seem to point to a christening, engagement, or wedding celebration—if this was the case then this event is pertinent and has relevance to your question. Perhaps you met someone there?

Most recently passing through, this would be in the past few weeks normally, it would seem you may have had to be diplomatic with somebody, as the card warns of diplomacy rather than aggressive responses.

Looking to the immediate future cards we are shown that a whole new cycle of events are coming into being, this card is known to bring good luck and destiny into play, with new beginnings and a whole new chapter in store. The important

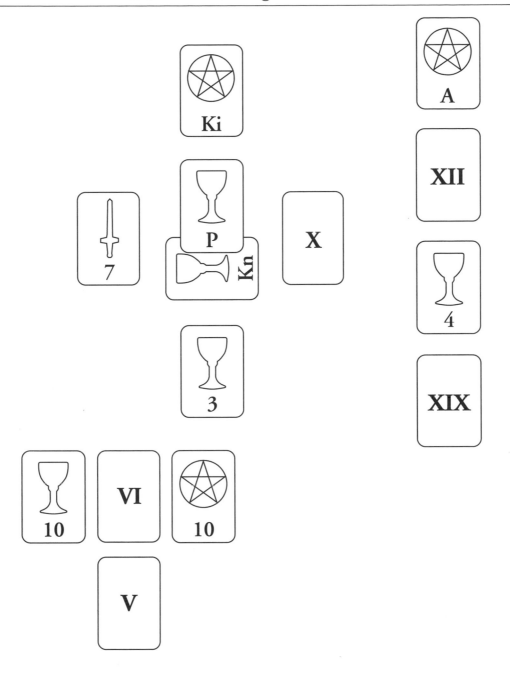

message of this card is that once the hand of fate turns the wheel we never know when it will be turned again—so strike whilst the iron is hot.

There are a number of elements in this reading that tend to make me wonder if there is someone around you whom you may have already dismissed out of hand, perhaps too hastily.

Firstly, we have the initial cards, and the future seems to lead to a contract (which may be a marriage contract) and the side reading also backs up a very serious and committed, loving relationship. But the way the other person (or other people) is looking at you shows that you appear disinterested. The Four of Cups shows a youth who has rather good circumstances yet when the heavens open and a hand offers a fourth and most beautiful cup, the youth looks nonchalant and disinterested. I sometimes call this card the one of divine discontent—nothing is actually wrong at all, just a feeling of it not being quite right either, but for no apparent reason.

Your thoughts here may lend a further clue, as we have a King of Pentacles offset with the Hanging Man. This again would tend to show that you are looking at someone but perhaps differently to everyone else—it also shows that perhaps a small sacrifice on your part needs to be made, in order to gain something of greater value. It may be that this person doesn't initially, in your eyes, "tick all the boxes," yet were you to look at this differently you could find you actually have what you want right in front of you.

The King of Pentacles is usually a very down to earth person, they work hard, are solid and reliable, trustworthy, and often methodical in their approach. Their vocation can be as diverse as being a banker, financier, successful businessman, farmer, tradesman, vet, food industries or jewels—all of which have an earth connection. This person may be an earth sign. But the biggest giveaway is usually their basic character, given at the beginning—very steadfast and loyal types, they can make wonderful partners.

I should also advise you that if you are feeling somewhat negative about this person then the cards are saying "Well, actually, no…this is very good and brings happiness," as we have the Sun.

For all the world, Pauline, with these cards I would think I am looking at someone already married—or about to be. I am sure this person is already around you, in your life, or may have already approached you. Now, isn't that intriguing?

So I feel there is plenty for you to ponder here...the answer to your question would appear to be yes—it's just that you may not have recognised them as actually being your "soul mate."

As always, I must remind you that the Tarot are a wonderful guide but they are not your master, only you can decide what is right for you, no one else has the responsibility for your actions or choices.

I do hope this is helpful to you and send my very best wishes for the future.

Love & Light,
Josie

First Impressions

My dilemma here was that as soon as I saw the cards I felt I was dealing with someone who was already married. The first three cards of the reading focus on what has already happened and is affecting the seeker in relation to their question. If you look at the Reader's Fan, it appeared quite adamant too.

As readers we are not judgemental, our task is to provide confidential guidance provided by the cards to the seeker. It is not unusual to find people in all manner of personal entanglements or tricky love relationship situations. Should they stay? Should they go? Is someone better out there for them? As any experienced reader could tell you, the computations of relationship situations are endless. When you are faced with certain cards and the seeker is sitting with you or on the other end of the telephone, you can tactfully question them before proceeding (without risking sticking your foot in it.) Email, however, is slightly different when you don't know the circumstances surrounding the question and, given the spread, it would be easy to cause offence by saying the wrong thing.

As you can see by my response, the cards and my instinct were so strong I had to mention to Pauline that I thought she was already married. How do you tactfully tell this to someone and that they already know their "soul mate" but have disregarded them, possibly out of hand? I did my best.

The useful experience of such situations, I believe, is reminding us to stay true to the messages the cards give and relaying them back to the seeker as given. Even when background information has been provided there are many instances where additional information has shown in the reading and, once related, was confirmed to be correct. This was despite it appearing to mean nothing earlier, or apparently being unrelated to the situation in question.

Pauline's Feedback

Pauline's reading was posted back to the site and I continued with other email readings that were scheduled for the day. Whilst online Pauline responded to my earlier message and our subsequent messages appear for you below:

> *Hello,*
> *I have just seen your message. I am married but the relationship is not going well and I am undecided how to proceed. My husband hasn't grown in over twenty years and I feel isolated within our relationship. I am unsure what other information may be helpful.*
> *Pauline*

> *Hi Pauline,*
> *I had already posted your reading earlier today ... so I think you might find it interesting! Please go back to your online reading page if you haven't done so already. Hope this helps.*
> *Josie*

> *Dear Josie,*
> *Thank you so much for my reading.*
> *I have now read it a few times and it has been very enlightening. I have recently purchased your set of book and cards, have tried to read Tarot in the past with little success; you have given me new inspiration. Once again thank you.*
> *Pauline*

The Main Indicators of the Reading

Cards 1, 2, 3, and 7

The Page of Cups is happy news of an emotional nature, the Knight of Cups brings offers and proposals of love and the history (card 3—Three of Cups) connected to the first card shows a wedding, due to the associations of the first two cards. Note the Sun in the apprehensions area: this card together with the third can also show some history to the situation, aside from its meaning as a future card. This tells us that the relationship has been good in the past. The first three cards are our starting point of the story, the background to the question. A proposal and a wedding are shown and have already taken place.

The Reader's Fan Cards: 11, 12, 13, and 14

On this occasion these cards could almost be heard screaming for recognition! How many indicators do we need to show an established, committed relationship, particularly with the Hierophant sat over the top of them? These cards confirmed the feelings from the first three cards.

Cards 5, 9, and 8

The King of Pentacles is the man in Pauline's subconscious (as it turned out, her husband). The card in the ninth position is a major card, with the fifth being only a minor the likelihood is that Pauline will lean more towards the energy of the ninth card. The eighth card represents how other people are viewing the situation—with the Four of Cups, this completes the picture.

A Year Later, the Conclusion

Just over a year later I wrote to Pauline to ask permission to reproduce her reading for the book and asked how things had turned out. Her response is given below:

> *Dear Josie*
> *I have no problem at all with you using my reading.*
> *At the time I did not realise just how little information I gave you. Time is a wonderful thing; you told me I had met my soul mate, still unsure what that actually means but we have slowly worked through our difficulties and our relationship is now better than it has ever been! Thank you so much,*
> *Pauline*

Phew…isn't it nice to have a happy ending?

Reader's Tips
Thoughts to Consider with Email Readings

If you are contemplating launching yourself online and doing readings by email from a website there are a few things you may wish to take into consideration before setting up.

Sometimes email readings can be very time consuming. Even when you have asked for a specific question or background details, often there are important areas not provided. It can create a lot of emails back and forth gathering information—or the seeker has some questions afterwards. Add this to the time to do the reading, and then typing it all up afterwards, etc. (For this reason it is easier to use smaller spreads.)

There are a number of ways you can personalise the reading in order to choose the cards. Some readers prefer the seeker to provide numbers, for instance, how many times the deck is shuffled and then a sequence of numbers (for the cards to be taken from the deck and used for the spread) from 1 to 78, to ascertain which cards are drawn, starting from the top of the deck for the reading. This is usually provided together with a question or questions. By using this method you may feel more confident that the cards drawn are of the seeker's choosing.

From my own website all members are now provided with a private area where they can upload their name, date of birth, photograph, and location. I ask for one specific question and only the *relevant* background details surrounding it, including dates of birth (if known) for anyone included in their question. This is to recognise the court card if it shows in the spread. Usually I will use the astrological signs associated with the courts for email readings, as it is quicker to establish. I shuffle the cards whilst focussing upon the seeker's photograph and reading the relevant information until I feel sufficiently attuned, then stop, cut the cards into three in the usual way, and lay out the spread. I am used to tuning into people in this way as it is how I work when providing distant healing, but it can take some concentration, so you may wish to experiment with both techniques until you find what works best for you.

If a set time has been promised for their reading to be returned, try not to keep people waiting—some people are still quite suspicious of the Internet and can be quite impatient, or think the worst when they have already paid you. Even when information is fully provided, some people do not read instructions either. After a couple of situations like this I became wiser but most was learned through trial and error.

There have been a couple of occasions where people have complained to the payment provider that they never received the service they paid for when their reading was on the site waiting, delivered within the appointed time and had been provided with clear instructions at the outset. Such situations can be messy and upsetting to sort out, but thankfully the site is set up so we can prove various points to the payment provider, should they arise. None of this applied to Pauline's reading, she simply hadn't seen the email, but it seemed an opportune moment to mention some of the finer details that can occur when working on the Internet.

The reason we have a private area on the site is that emails may be bounced by overfilled in-boxes or wrapped up in overzealous spam filters—if this happens a few times you can become blacklisted ... and that can be awkward to sort out. All this in addition to whether you were provided the correct email address to begin with. I have spoken to a number of other readers and those with busy sites agree that email can produce some annoying problems.

It is worth talking to a professional web designer first. It is not always as straightforward as we would all like, and if you have a very busy site these problems can become magnified. Giving these areas some thought beforehand could save you a few headaches later.

On the positive side, if your site and facility are clearly thought out, it is possible to read for a whole host of people from around the world who otherwise would not have access to you.

7
The Silent Client

my lives in Scotland and contacted me through my website to ask for a reading. I was unavailable at the time (I was writing this book), but since she was a new client, I invited her for a personal appointment if she would consider allowing us to publish her reading.

Amy begins by telling me she has previously had a reading with a psychic medium who used Tarot cards. I am especially careful to ensure she understands I will need some feedback as we progress, that I won't be working "cold," as a number of psychics or mediums prefer to do, and how the reading may differ. I let Amy know I will ask her questions as we go through the reading but to begin, I just need some basic information such as her age, marital status, children, and if she is working.

Amy smiles slightly but views me cautiously and crosses her arms. Her closed body language is not a good sign, but she could just be nervous, having never met me before. The information Amy provides me with is that she is not married, in her mid-thirties, with two children and is currently working, although not in the profession for which she qualified. Amy shuffles and cuts the cards and I cannot fail to notice that she promptly folds her arms again.

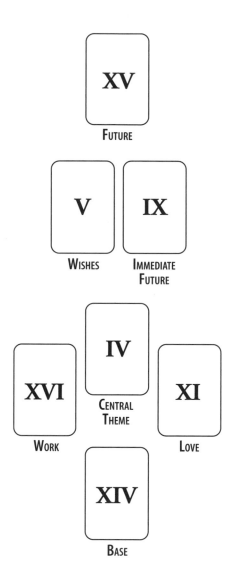

The Silent Client—Life Spread

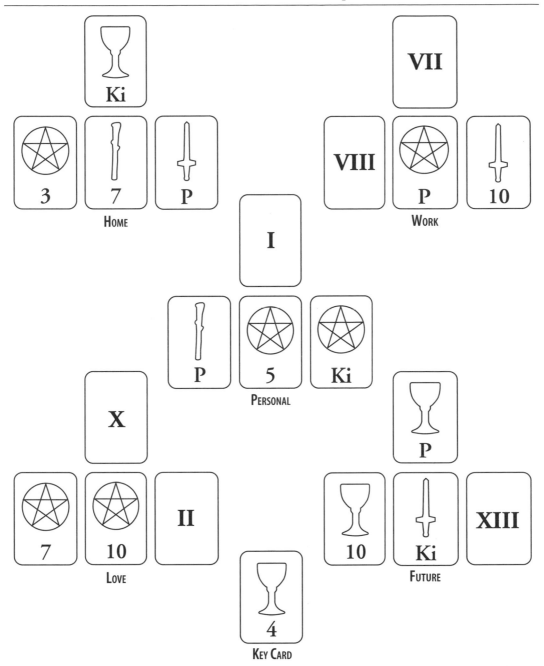

First Impressions

- The Tower in the work area of the Anchor and Ten of Swords at the end of the work area in the Life Spread.
- Justice in the love area of the Anchor, King of Swords with the Death card in the future area of the Life Spread.
- Three kings in different areas of the Life Spread.
- All four pages, none of which are attached to good news.
- Focus of the reading appears to be upon work and Cups are quite lacking.
- Three tens, indicating a transitional period leading to completion.
- Overall, the spreads appeared to have a disruptive influence running throughout.

The Anchor
FOUNDATION POSITION: TEMPERANCE
LOVE AREA: JUSTICE

I explain to Amy that our first card of the reading is usually quite harmonious and I ask if there has been a reconciliation of a relationship. Confirmation comes in the form of a positive monosyllable. I ask if this is quite recently and if it is a love relationship, further confirmed with a straightforward yes.

Moving across to Justice, I point out that the card in the area relating to love and relationships tends to suggest that she has been looking at this from a logical and rational perspective, as this is quite a practical card, rather than emotive. Another yes from Amy. I am quietly wondering if she has taken what I have said quite literally and if the reading is going to be like this throughout. She is very still and quiet but I have the information we need and hope she will become more relaxed as we progress.

The Anchor
WORK AREA: THE TOWER
The Life Spread
PERSONAL AREA: THE MAGICIAN, PAGE OF WANDS,
FIVE OF PENTACLES, KING OF PENTACLES
WORK AREA: THE CHARIOT, STRENGTH,
PAGE OF PENTACLES, TEN OF SWORDS

With the Tower in the work placement of the Anchor, the Ten of Swords at the end of the Life Spread work area, and the Five of Pentacles in the personal area, I decide to investigate Amy's current work position. Since the future shows an ending and disappointment of some kind, I don't want to alarm her if she is really not expecting it. It is more *how* I am going to approach her with the information that I am concerned about at this stage.

I ask if she is planning to leave her current employment. Amy says, "Eventually." But the cards I am looking at do not appear to indicate that type of circumstance. You may think I am skirting around the issue, but when I deliver the news, I want to know how prepared she is for it and how the cards best fit her position.

Quietly, I am also observing the cards in the personal area, since it appears that she will receive news with a work connection, resulting in some kind of financial loss or hardship. Following the cards' natural order, the King of Pentacles should follow the situation from the Five but it is possible he is connected to it. I ask if her employer is aware of this but Amy says no. I explain that the reason I ask is because the cards are showing an ending that is somehow work related but normally they would suggest that she is on the receiving end of the news, rather than the one delivering it, if she follows me, and it may not be in the timeframe she was expecting. So I have raised the issue but not fully delved into it, as yet.

I inform Amy that there are three men showing in her reading, possibly in different areas of her life, and so we are not second-guessing who they may be I would like to run through some descriptions with her in a moment. Amy agrees.

Staying with the work theme from the Chariot and Strength, I say that I can see she is working hard and determinedly and perhaps there is an element of learning here too. Another yes from Amy. The Chariot shows that she is keeping her energies in one direction and although there may be difficulties along the way she needs to try and stay focussed, as this card provides the strength to overcome obstacles she may encounter. Alongside this we also have Strength itself, a card of quiet determination, so I feel these two together back one another up and, since they are both from the major arcana, they are very powerful cards for her. Of course, it also means that a good deal of determination and resolve are required, which doesn't always point to an easy situation.

I briefly explain to Amy that "arcana" means secrets and point out the major and minor cards in the work area explaining that, whilst they are both important, the major cards tend to have more influence. I pass the Strength card to Amy so that she has to unfold her arms and then she leans forward to investigate the other images I am showing her. By explaining the cards in a little more detail and inviting her interaction I now feel happier that she seems more engaged in her reading. Closed body language, for whatever reason, whether defensive, protective, or nervous, always acts like a barrier, as subconsciously that is its purpose. The sooner you can remove closed body language the more relaxed and comfortable the atmosphere becomes between you and the seeker.

The Three Kings

In trying to identify the three kings I run through the personality descriptions for each. However, one confusing aspect is that the King of Pentacles and the King of Cups both appear with work-related cards. Even though the King of Cups appears as the Key card in Amy's home area there are still work-related cards here and there must be a reason for the card's positioning. With the exception of the future, all the other areas of the Life Spread appear to relate to work or finance. Amy decides the King of Cups is not her partner but, from the description and the fact there is a work connection, she states that there is an easy-going and creative man that calls into her place of work daily.

Amy cannot place the King of Pentacles being connected to her work but from the description given she asks if this would cover stockbrokers. I say that it would, but if she has shares he might not be bringing very good news. Amy says that she doesn't have any financial association with him but she knows someone personally that fits this description. Then she completely floors me by asking if royalty would count (this is not a question I am asked often!) I agree that it would. Amy says she knows him through work, although doesn't work for him. Had that been the case, I am sure this case study would not have found its way into the book— but it made for an interesting moment in the reading! You just never know.

The King of Swords draws a blank. I have covered his personality and that he may be connected to uniforms or the law but she still cannot place him, aside from some of the negative aspects of her current partner. I do not feel convinced, as by covering her partner's characteristics it would appear he is a King of Wands and, interestingly, the only king not present in the reading.

I am beginning to wish I had covered the kings in each area as we encountered them since I am not much wiser about their placements. I sometimes find this is the best approach to take, as otherwise people can try to "make" people they know fit into the reading. There is usually no mistake when the seeker recognises someone they know in the descriptions given, however, in this case I wonder if it may have been the wrong approach. Two of the kings could as yet be unknown to Amy, since they both occupy future positions.

The Life Spread
PERSONAL AREA: THE MAGICIAN, PAGE OF WANDS, FIVE OF PENTACLES, KING OF PENTACLES

Back to the drawing board! I start to cover the progression in the personal area. The Magician as the first card of the spread carries the message of having confidence in her talents and ability, mastering skills through concentration and will and then applying them, in order to succeed. As I am still trying to find my bearings on where we are in Amy's journey, I ask her if this card is relevant to her current circumstances. After another monosyllabic response, I ask if she can expand on that and briefly tell me why, so I can establish which cards apply to the past or present before moving onto the future.

Amy tells me that she had decided to go back to college to further her professional training; she views her regular work as a temporary measure whilst she retrains in her original vocation which she intends to pursue once the course is completed. Since the Page of Pentacles is central to her work area this card would fit perfectly with her further learning. I ask if she has very long to go to qualify; Amy says it will be finished shortly. The Ten of Swords should be connected to this but I am thrown by the fact that she is finishing soon, and together with the Tower from the Anchor, it is not the kind of situation that would suggest the natural end of her course.

I explain this to Amy and that the Page of Pentacles fits well to the fact she is following an educational course but normally the Ten of Swords brings an end that can be considered disappointing. With the Tower in her work-related area of the Anchor, this appears to be matters outside of her control but I cannot see how it fits into her situation. Whilst she may be expecting her course to end, the cards tend to suggest an ending of a different variety. As it is a refresher course for her, it is also unlikely she is going to fail because she is already qualified. I tell her that at the moment I cannot be clearer about this. The Page of Pentacles would usually naturally connect to her course but logically it doesn't seem to make a great deal of sense. This could instead highlight the financial side found in the interpretation of this card, which would also connect to the Five of Pentacles following the Page of Wands in the personal area.

The Page of Wands usually brings positive news connected to work but since this is followed by the Five of Pentacles it would appear it might not be so happy on this occasion. As the Five of Pentacles is normally associated to financial loss I can only assume it must be connected to her paying job. And then we have the King of Pentacles, who still remains a mystery. Amy tells me she is sure it is her stockbroker friend, although I am not sure how he connects to the situation so decide to come back to this later.

The Life Spread
HOME AREA: KING OF CUPS, THREE OF PENTACLES, SEVEN OF WANDS, PAGE OF SWORDS

Work further dominates this area with the Three of Pentacles showing work that Amy is good at and has natural ability, for which she may also receive recognition. The Seven of Wands tells us that she feels very strongly about this, and she may feel challenged enough to stand up for her principles, ideals, and beliefs, but can do so with confidence.

Amy reports that she feels this relates to her studies, as she feels quite passionate about her subject, whereas when she originally trained this was not the case. The Page of Swords could bring delays to the conclusion, or some news she may consider disappointing. I explain that we now have three pages indicating some form of disappointing news connected to her career in some way, so it seems likely they may all point to the same incident.

I refer back to the King of Cups, the Key card in the home area whom Amy does not associate with her partner, but someone who visits her daily at work. His position in this area is also a little mysterious.

The Life Spread
RELATIONSHIP AREA: WHEEL OF FORTUNE, SEVEN OF PENTACLES, TEN OF PENTACLES, THE HIGH PRIESTESS

This area almost appears to contradict the other indications of financial loss, I feel that it may, perhaps, provide a certain level of protection. The Wheel tends to indicate there has been a change and usually for the better, suggesting the commencement of a new cycle or chapter in life. Amy says this makes sense to her.

With the Seven of Pentacles, I feel as if this is where Amy probably is right now, with its message of readiness to collect the harvest after the period of hard work that has gone beforehand. Being followed by the Ten of Pentacles these two cards strengthen the message of material gain. The Wheel of Fortune appearing with these two cards certainly appears to highlight financial matters in a very positive way, and could bring the sense of a lucky break into the equation, although the High Priestess seems to indicate some form of secrecy surrounding it.

The Ten of Pentacles is also the card of stability in the home and is associated with family. As there can be a property connection with this card, it usually symbolises the family home. The High Priestess adds to the sense of mystery that seems to have followed a pattern of the last card in each area! Information or secrets should be revealed to Amy that will be to her benefit here. Outside of this the High Priestess tells us very little, for that is her purpose in some respects. Representing the gatekeeper of the veil and a level of higher information we cannot access without her support or assistance in some way, she does not reveal her secrets to us easily until she feels we are ready to receive it. I find it interesting that it can also represent work of a more caring nature, which is in fact the opposite side of the coin from the paid work Amy is currently doing, representing instead the vocation she intends to return to.

Whilst interpretations may fit current circumstances, these are future indications. Experience reminds me that these cards relate to future aspects. Since the High Priestess follows the Seven and Ten of Pentacles, it must be connected to this situation in some way, so what it reveals will be in relation to them.

As stated earlier, this seems to be at complete odds with the messages of financial loss, even the possible loss that is indicated in the work areas. Due to this I feel that somehow Amy will be protected but because it is the High Priestess I cannot tell her how. The secrecy aspect of the High Priestess is interesting because the Devil, in the future of the Anchor, can also represent secret plans. It could be that Amy has secret plans of her own. She hasn't said so, but then again so far she has said very little.

Since both the High Priestess and the Devil occupy future positions, the message of secrecy is doubled and seems to highlight this aspect of the interpretation for the future in some way. Seems like the future is something of a secret—how frustrating for a reader that is!

The Anchor
IMMEDIATE FUTURE: THE HERMIT
The Life Spread
IMMEDIATE FUTURE: THE PAGE OF CUPS, TEN OF CUPS,
KING OF SWORDS, DEATH

In the immediate future of the Anchor, the Hermit shows that Amy is approaching a period where she may be taking some quiet time for soul-searching and contemplation regarding her future.

At first glance the future area of the Life Spread appears to be another contradiction in terms. The Page of Cups usually brings good news of an emotional nature, with the Ten of Cups this skyrockets up the emotional league, being the card of happiness in the heart department. The King of Swords must be connected, as he follows the Ten and is centrally situated but then we have the Death card bringing a major end. This was the reason why I wanted to try and identify who the King of Swords was with Amy, if she already knows him, before reaching this section. Since we have been unable to definitely pinpoint him, it presents us with something of a cliffhanger, and the dilemma of which way to apply the cards. So let's break it down.

One possibility may be that the King of Swords is the reason for the Ten of Cups and leads to the ending of Amy's existing relationship. Had this card been Amy's partner it would then appear more likely that he would be the one ending the relationship and these cards would then seem more fitting to that scenario. However, looking at this group of cards logically it is perhaps the Page that is causing the confusion, not the following three, although this doesn't help us identify the King of Swords. Due to the Death card, which is also the only major card of the group, it could be that the emotional news the page brings is not good.

However, if we follow the progression just as it is in front of us, and with the presence of the Death card we could keep the Page more neutral. Also, perhaps the key lies in the major cards in the Anchor, which we haven't really referenced.

My first description with the King of Swords I covered with Amy is that this man may be connected to uniforms or the law. With the Ten starting this progression it points us in the direction of relationships, and in the love area of the Anchor we have Justice, strongly associated with legal dealings. The King of Swords could be a solicitor (the British equivalent to a lawyer), or legally connected. If the King of Swords were another relationship I would have expected the Ten of Cups to follow him; this is not always the case, but it is usually quite reliable to follow the progression given by the cards. So based on this it would appear that Amy could be the one bringing this relationship to an end. Also, if we look at the other cards yet emerging in the Anchor, the Hermit and the Devil are not what we would expect if she were happily disappearing off into the great blue yonder with a new love; they're not conducive with a Ten of Cups moment. So, in this instance it would seem we are looking at an ending rather than a major change of, let us say, a more positive variety.

I explain to Amy that I am really of two minds about the King of Swords; one of the reasons I wanted to pinpoint his identity early on. Amy looks at the cards thoughtfully for a moment and then asks, "You say there are three men around me in the reading?" She smiles at me a little coyly. I ask if this is significant to her. After her standard yes response, I start laughing with her and say she is going to have enlighten me further on this now. Finally, Amy starts talking to me.

She has been with her partner for a number of years and he actually lives with her but is not emotionally supportive—he is hot-tempered and violence has featured in the relationship previously (my eyes take in the Devil at the top of the reading). In many ways she says she feels they are detached from the relationship and each other. She goes on to say that the cards in her love area are very accurate because she was seriously ill for a long period of time, unable to work or earn, so the Wheel of Fortune and Seven of Pentacles very much represented what she was doing in her life, trying to stabilise her future home life for herself and the children. Whilst she understood the message of the High Priestess was still to come, it was her illness that made her want to return to her trained vocation, due to the caring aspect within it, so in many ways the cards in this area fit to her present situation as well. So, the High Priestess could represent her secret plans in the future.

She thinks the King of Pentacles is someone she used to see, the one with the financial dealings. He still keeps in touch with her and when he took her out he treated her extremely well. He would still take her out if she was willing, but she never knows where she is with him because she always feels as if the relationship is rather noncommittal.

The King of Cups is so different from her partner—kind, caring, thoughtful, and creative—that she finds his whole nature very appealing and interesting. Were it not for her circumstances, she would like to investigate whether there could be a proper relationship with him and pursue it. She finds herself thinking about him all the time.

Since Amy's entire vocabulary contribution had been one word, or a single sentence when necessary, it is helpful for me to see how various areas of the reading fit her current circumstances. She never tried to deceive me and she did supply me with the information I needed as I asked for it (it appears she took me at my word initially!). However, in certain ways I am now pleased that the interaction in the reading has progressed the way it did. It is also a relief that finally the dots seem to connect and makes sense to some of the various placements of the cards. It strikes me that the King of Cups is like her "crowning thoughts" in her home area, and how accurate that is. With the sense of detachment, it perhaps also explains why her partner's card is the only male court card not showing in her reading.

Before verbalising my thoughts to Amy I want to test the waters with her first, in case this is news she may not be expecting, so I ask in the positive, "You haven't been thinking of ending this relationship by any chance, have you?" To which Amy replies yes. I go on to explain that it is possible that the King of Swords could be a new person entering the scene, however, I feel it is more likely that he represents the law, uniforms, or a solicitor, as since they live together one would be required. Amy explains that if she breaks up with him she thinks it could involve both the police and a solicitor, as the police were needed before; and she anticipates him becoming violent.

For all that Amy has explained to me now and even though she feels the cards fit various aspects of her life they don't feel right to me. It is the way the cards have presented themselves, the order in which they have appeared and those appearing alongside. For me as a reader, it all doesn't quite gel. I feel as if I am still grappling about somewhat, with bits of information not quite within my grasp.

The Anchor
CENTRAL POSITION: THE EMPEROR
The Life Spread
KEY CARD: FOUR OF CUPS

Once again we find two cards that appear to oppose one another in certain ways, yet given the circumstances surrounding Amy they make quite a lot of sense. On the one hand we have the strength of purpose that the Emperor provides: a logical, rational card, often associated with ambition and our standing in life. Alternatively, we have the rather blasé attitude of the Four of Cups, suggesting a kind of nonchalance to what surrounds her. But I feel this is very true as to how Amy is handling her circumstances.

Characteristic to the nature of the card, she shrugs as she likens her relationship to a security blanket. While it isn't right, she knows how it operates and has found a way of feeling safe within it. Until she is ready to make changes, she says she's fine with how things are, and shrugs again. I look at the Four of Cups (you couldn't make it up if you tried) and realise her image will remain with me connected to the card because she typified everything it conveys so well!

Amy did feel the Emperor represents her ambition found through her studies, that which drives her on and provides the sense of purpose and future of her life. As the central card, everything else revolves around it, so it certainly holds her life together and is her main focus.

I explain to Amy that she seems to have a number of endings coming up in various areas of her life, but from what she has told me she doesn't appear to be fazed by them. I suggest that this could be due to her previous illness, as I have noticed from others in similar circumstances; once they have faced a major illness, their attitude to what life throws at them is often viewed in a different perspective. Amy says this is quite true and she doesn't feel worried from what the reading has revealed so far.

The Anchor
HOPES AND WISHES: THE HIEROPHANT
FUTURE: THE DEVIL

Interestingly, in Amy's hopes and wishes section I tell her that from the Hierophant I feel that she would really like to be married and happily settled, living her life in quite a traditional, conventional way. Amy smiles and says this is very true.

I explain that the Devil has a variety of meanings that could be relevant to her situation; it could suggest she is heading towards a period where she may feel dragged down by a situation she feels enslaved to in some way, although this can also represent a controlling or manipulative relationship. However, the Devil can also be an empowering card as it does remind us that we are only enslaved so long as we are prepared to remain so. In other words, we can release the chains and walk away whenever we feel ready to do so, thereby regaining control of a situation. As the Devil is the card of secret plans, and since the Hermit precedes it, it could also show that these belong to Amy.

I explain to Amy that I do not feel entirely sure about the connection of the King of Pentacles to the financial loss and ask why she feels so sure it is the man she knows. Since he is not connected to her work and he doesn't represent her financial interests, why would he be connected to the financial loss? Amy laughs as she explains that he is a successful businessman with diverse interests, but his primary business handles bankruptcy cases, so financial loss is what he deals with. Fancy that!

As enlightening as this may be, and whilst this man may feature in her life, I tell Amy I cannot be sure it is this friend, unless perhaps he is going to be helpful to her in some way. It is always difficult when a court card is the last card of the trio and appears to be unrelated. Similar to the tenth position placement in the Celtic Cross, it tends to inform us that this person will be important in some way in the future. So we will need to see how that one unfolds in due course.

I confirm with Amy that the cards currently indicate the possibility of an ending connected to work and a further ending connected to relationships. Whilst there is the warning of financial loss, the cards appear to show she is protected in some way. However, I suggest it may be wise to be careful with her finances for the moment, so she doesn't get caught short. We can see that major changes feature in her life but Amy seems prepared for them and says she is very pleased with her reading.

And so my initially silent seeker whisks away into the night and off towards her future, all smiles. I am warmed by her positive attitude in her circumstances and sincerely hope things work out well for her.

Results and Feedback

Five Months Later

When I finally heard from Amy, it appeared most of her results had manifested within a four-month period and the way they did was quite interesting. Without recounting the cards in the various areas, I will let you see for yourself how her situation connected to them.

Amy encountered a difficult situation at the end of her course: an instructor used her as the subject for a practical examination but unfortunately had not considered the contra-indications, which resulted in a medical problem relating to Amy's previous illness. She landed in the hospital.

Aside from her obvious upset, Amy stated she was further annoyed when the tutor responsible at her college had informed her it would not be wise to officially complain if she wanted to receive her course certification. To add insult to injury, Amy had also received the bill for the final part of her college course.

Now what I didn't know was that Amy was using a private provider. I had wrongly assumed she meant her local college, so I never asked pertinent questions during the reading. Given her age, it stood to reason that a fee would have been involved—private or otherwise. As the provider was private, the sum was substantial.

Amy felt a strong sense of injustice and decided to call the college head office; the person she was referred to was equally appalled by her experience. She was informed it would not affect her qualifying certificate and they would not expect her to pay the final installment for the course.

Following this incident and the latest setback to her health, it was in fact her titled friend (King of Pentacles) who offered to provide financial backing for her new business. Amy had been taken aback by his generosity but was giving the matter consideration, on the understanding that she would pay a percentage back to one of his charities, so she felt she would be helping someone else in return. However, since areas of her new business remain under wraps, none of this is public knowledge yet.

When asked about her love life, Amy reported that some information had come to light concerning her partner and she felt it was the final straw. She told me she was just biding her time, as she had plans she needed to implement in order to leave in the future. One aspect that had shocked her was that her parents' marriage ended and this was quite unexpected because she thought they were happy. Amy said her father was a military man.

I wouldn't have considered that scenario but it does make sense, since Amy was not experiencing the Ten of Cups within her own life. It is still possible that the King of Swords may connect to the legal side of bringing her own partnership to an end in the future—as the contents of the reading could still apply for a further seven months and it does feature in her forward plans. However, since everything else in her reading is complete, and the Devil in the final position connects to the secrecy surrounding Amy's future plans, I believe that the information the reading supplied us with may now be complete.

Reader's Tips
Delivering Bad News

The Tower, Death, the Ten of Swords, and (to a lesser extent) the Devil are all cards most of us would prefer not to encounter when they occupy a future position, let alone be faced with the full monty! In Amy's reading there were also some saving graces to counterbalance bad news, but these cards are never easy to discuss and most of us don't relish having to cover them.

Life is not always hunky-dory and whilst the Life Spread and Anchor may provide the opportunity to focus upon more positive aspects of the reading, a question posed to the Celtic Cross with one of the biggies in position 10 puts us in a difficult spot. Unfortunately, we cannot always deliver the good news that people want to hear, no matter how much we wish to, and glossing over what is in front of us is not a very honest policy either. So how do we deal with it?

Take a gentle approach and be as diplomatic as possible, but also help the seeker recognise that sometimes life just doesn't go the way we would like. We can remind them that whilst it may not be the answer they were hoping for, we are only looking at a small part of the larger landscape of their life; a captured moment in a lifetime. Life is constantly evolving and changing, bringing new people and opportunities into play all the time if they can remain open to new experiences.

If the seeker asks the question and disappointing cards appear, we would be failing them if we did not advise them properly on what we see. At least in our honesty we can present the opportunity for them to focus their energy in a more favourable direction, rather than dressing up disappointment in a false rosy glow. It is possible that once forewarned they could try a different approach to their problem, which may help to avoid the direction the cards show. They could also pursue a different avenue that may provide a more beneficial outcome.

We can soften the blow and we may not see all the circumstances surrounding the situation, but when things don't look very promising it is best to say so as kindly as possible. By discussing the different options that may be available, the Tarot could then be used to address another question, therefore helping them find an alternative solution. If we were not honest, would they trust us next time?

The Cowboy

*R*eid L. Rosenthal is president of a number of companies primarily involved in ranching, resource enhancement and conservation, land management, and limited development in certain special areas. His expertise spans more than forty years, and he has worked successfully with thousands of ranches across North and South America. Alongside his passion for land preservation, Reid also writes, something he has pursued more seriously in the last few years with a number of works in the pipeline. Reid is in his fifties, divorced, with two children, and spends his time divided among his ranches in the west.

I have never read for Reid before and this will be the first time he has ever had a Tarot reading. Although we have shared letters for a number of years I cannot say I have an in-depth knowledge of his private life or business dealings, as it's a bit tricky with the Atlantic in between! Our mail has mainly focussed upon shared passions, our differing landscapes, and writing, indulging our respective weakness for descriptive prose. You will find Reid mentioned in the "Acknowledgements" section of my first book, which I wrote following my stay at his ranches more than five years ago. Due to the aforementioned distance, this was a telephone reading.

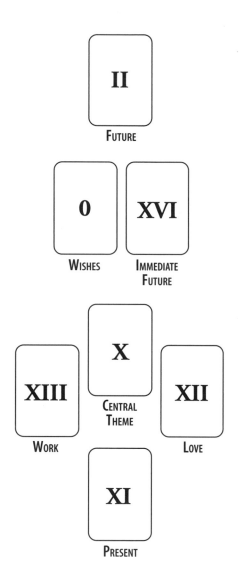

The Cowboy—Life Spread

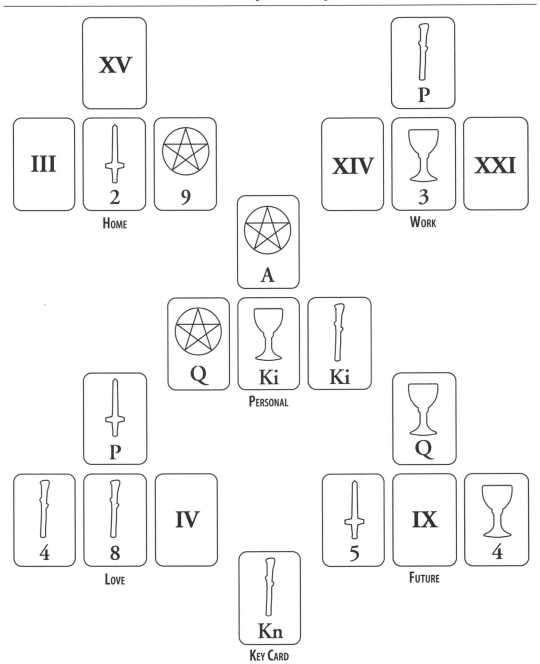

First Impressions

- Major change seems poised with Death and the Tower in the Anchor, although this is not reflected negatively in the Life Spread. The Wheel is the central theme of the Anchor and the Fool also shows his wish for change.

- The three court cards together in the personal area of the Life Spread connected to the Ace of Pentacles.

- The Life Spread appears quite well balanced of the four suits overall but majors and courts provide the single greatest numbers.

The Anchor
PRESENT POSITION: JUSTICE

Starting the reading from Justice in the present position of the Anchor, I ask Reid if important legal papers, contracts, or agreements currently surround him. He states that with the many diverse aspects of his business he is constantly involved in legal contracts and agreements of a varying nature. I explain that the other meaning of this card suggests that he may also be looking at aspects of his life from a very logical point of view at present. Reid agrees that both interpretations would be accurate.

The Life Spread
PERSONAL AREA: ACE OF PENTACLES, QUEEN OF PENTACLES, KING OF CUPS, KING OF WANDS

Moving straight across to the personal area of the Life Spread, the Ace of Pentacles as the first card of the main reading may also suggest important documents of material relevance regarding land and property, making a link with Justice. This appears to involve three people, or where a number of people will feature prominently. None of the court cards represent Reid, whom I consider to be the King of Pentacles, as a successful businessman with land and property interests.

The Queen of Pentacles may be involved with land or property or she could be connected to finance however the personality traits would describe her as methodical with attention to detail. The King of Cups is a man of easy-going nature, one who does not usually attract enemies and is generally well liked; he may be connected to a caring profession or creative endeavours. The King of Wands has quite a different temperament to the King of Cups, appearing more dynamic and often with an entrepreneurial leaning; they dislike details, preferring to "just get on with it" and can thus seem to have a more impulsive nature.

From the descriptions given, Reid cannot place them all in one particular transaction; he explains that he is usually involved with multiple deals and consequently, a number of various people simultaneously. Since some of the properties are bought or sold as consortiums, defining particular individuals to one specific deal is not easy. At the moment, he feels the first individual may be relevant but cannot place the other two. I point out it's possible he may not have come into contact with all parties involved as yet, since the cards usually move into the future. That said, the cards create quite an accurate picture of his work.

I tell Reid that I believe the court cards must be of particular relevance since they are the first cards of the reading and are in his personal area. I inform him we will leave it for the moment and come back to it later, as the difficulty is that whilst the court cards provide descriptions of people, I have no further action with which to connect them. It's possible there could be other indications elsewhere in the reading. However, I do feel that all three of these people must in some way be related to this document and it must have particular significance to him, due to their presence. It is also possible that since we have nothing but courts in this area, the cards are showing us a situation that involves many other people.

The Anchor
Work Area: Death
The Life Spread
Work Area: Page of Wands, Temperance, Three of Cups, The World

The Death card signifies major change in the work area of the Anchor and should close a chapter to enable a new one to begin. I ask Reid if there is anything that has recently come to an end in his work area. In connection with work he says he is in the process of finalising various deals. However, I tell him I feel it is more relevant than this and had it already happened he would be more aware of it, so I think it is still to come. I explain that the other cards in his work area look very good so although it may be a major change, it appears to be a positive one.

The Page of Wands as the Key card in the work area of the Life Spread signifies happy news or messages connected to work should have already been received—if not it is soon to follow. Temperance may show a situation that has possibly gone on for a while as it represents patience or a situation that has required patience and diplomacy on his part. As a card of balanced emotions and healing, it can represent successfully integrating opposite forces, harmoniously combining energies, which can sometimes suggest reconciliation, and perhaps a further indication of something long-standing. The Three of Cups brings an abundance of good feeling, emotional growth, happiness, and cause for celebration. The World at the end of this trio shows a successful conclusion and triumphant achievement, not usually of the overnight variety.

Overall, the three cards seem to link very well, as if speaking in a sentence to one particular situation. I feel the situation, whatever it may be, is outside Reid's usual dealings, as the cards seem too personal (there are plenty of success cards that could show connected purely to successful business endeavours). Temperance and the Three of Cups are not what I would normally expect to see. Together with the Death card from the Anchor, they will bring about some kind of major change.

At this point Reid informs me he is currently in the process of remarketing the home ranch. The sale would definitely bring about a major change in his work area as his personal offices are situated at the ranch and, although he has other offices, it would change the setup of his business. Again, this is an area I want to return to, once we have investigated the cards a little more.

The Life Spread
HOME AREA: THE DEVIL, THE EMPRESS,
TWO OF SWORDS, NINE OF PENTACLES
The Life Spread
KEY CARD: KNIGHT OF WANDS

The Devil in the home area suggests either secret plans or feeling mired in a situation. With the Empress as the first card, it indicates that this is in connection with something that Reid has been nurturing for quite some time connected to the home. The Two of Swords represents a stalemate or deadlock, a position that he may currently feel he cannot move out of, a frustration the Devil seems to echo.

Reid says he feels this also relates to the sale of the home ranch. I tell him that if this is the case, three areas of the cards are now reflecting it as such. Although I understand it is a big move and would be of particular importance to him, I am not so sure all the cards are related to this one aspect of his life. Even though all the cards would fit the current situation there is a danger of missing other important issues that may not be on the radar yet.

I feel these cards are connected to the sale, primarily because it is his home area and they do relate to the situation well. The spectacular custom-built property in the mountains has been his home for many years and the centre of Reid's business operations, as well as the home where he raised his children. The Empress, as the card of nurturing, is also reflective of the enormous care that has gone into every aspect of the ranch and land, involving years of careful planning and development.

Reid says that the economic downturn has slowed down his plans to move and although he has mentally moved on and could physically go ahead if he wished, he feels the description reflects his current feelings about the matter. As the Two of Swords is the central card, I tell him he may experience the feeling of deadlock for a little while longer but the Nine of Pentacles (the card of financial increase through one's own efforts) suggests the property should sell in the future.

The Knight of Wands as the Key card of the Life Spread may also show a change of residence. Since for Reid this is not simply a change of home perhaps it explains the significance of it being the Key card of the Life Spread. Another interesting aspect of this card is that Reid travels extensively and lives between two of his ranches, something I was not aware of until the time of the reading.

The Life Spread
Personal and Work Areas

Moving back to the personal and work areas both could relate to the situation concerning the home ranch. In my own cards, the Ace of Pentacles has often represented my manuscript or book and since Reid writes, I feel it may also connect to this area of his life.

With regards to his manuscripts he works with a female editor, a successful published author in her own right. This Queen of Pentacles "dots the 'i's' and crosses the 't's'"—a phrase I often use for Pentacle types due to their methodical attention to detail. The King of Cups can also represent creative types, so the following two kings could be important in his quest for publication.

Temperance, the Three of Cups, and the World may also fit into his author activities. Reid has always wanted to write seriously and studied journalism as one of his majors in college. As is often the case, life tends to take over while sleeping ambitions lie just beneath the surface, but over the last few years Reid has seriously turned his attention to writing a number of books, starting a website and blog to feature his writing and is collecting quite an online following. I feel these three cards would be representative of how he would feel if he achieved success with his writing or was accepted for publishing, as the World is the card to look for when realising important ambitions. Temperance is the card of patience, aside from the lengthy job of putting a work together, writers are also alchemists but with words, searching and blending for the perfect combination.

The Death card would also be important here, as Reid would like to scale back his business operations and focus more upon his writing ambitions. This would represent a major change but the home ranch is also an important part of this process.

Whilst all the cards could relate to the ranch sale I feel it is always worth covering the different interpretations the cards can show. (As we have seen from some of the other case studies, it is surprising how often they may all be relevant.) I explain to Reid that we can ask more specific questions in a moment if he wishes.

The Anchor
LOVE AREA: THE HANGING MAN
The Life Spread
RELATIONSHIP AREA: PAGE OF SWORDS, FOUR OF SWORDS, EIGHT OF WANDS, THE EMPEROR

With the Hanging Man I ask if he has been reassessing his love life lately or reconsidering it from a different viewpoint, as if stepping back and perceiving it differently. Reid says this is accurate. Moving across to the Life Spread love area I ask if he has had some news recently that he would consider slightly disappointing, or if there had been delays getting something off the ground. Reid says nothing comes to mind.

Since this doesn't immediately resonate with him I try working with the meanings of the cards as given, linking the Four of Swords to the Page as a continuation. The Hanging Man shows that perhaps he has stepped out of the frame to reassess matters. The Four of Swords also showing a period of inactivity or withdrawal, tending to amplify the delaying aspect of the Page interpretation. The other overlapping interpretation of suspension from the Hanging Man also strengthens the interpretation found in the Page and Four of Swords. Translated this becomes a situation that has encountered delays that he may have considered disappointing (Page of Swords), resulting in a period of withdrawal or inactivity to re-gather thoughts (Four of Swords) producing a period of reassessment following suspension of plans (Hanging Man). Reid says this makes sense to him but does not enlighten me further.

I inform him that whatever this situation may be it appears set to change quite rapidly. The Eight of Wands brings exciting good news coming in swiftly; the pace of events may speed up and travel may also be connected. (The Eight of Wands often represents speed after what may have previously been a stagnant period, which also ties in very well with the previously mentioned cards of this area.) Reid starts to laugh, but I have been concentrating and wonder if I must have missed the joke somewhere.

With the Emperor concluding this scenario it will place him in quite a powerful position. As a card that represents leadership, authority, and ambition, it tends to suggest that he will be the one taking the lead here. It shows that he will be looking at this situation with reason and logic, although it could lead to stability in his love life in the future. Overall, these are positive and encouraging cards although the Emperor is an ambitious and very logical card to have at the end of a love area.

The Anchor
CENTRAL POSITION: THE WHEEL OF FORTUNE
IMMEDIATE FUTURE: THE TOWER
HOPES AND WISHES: THE FOOL

As the central card around which all the others revolve the Wheel of Fortune is a positive sign representing a positive change of fortune and the beginning of a new chapter with a new cycle commencing. The Wheel often brings a sense of fate and fortune when Lady Luck or the hand of destiny steps into play, representing the external forces of the Universe providing the opportunity to capitalise on a stroke of good luck.

There are some fairly major change cards showing here; with Death in the work area and the Tower in the immediate future, changes could be fairly radical. However, note the Fool in Reid's wishes position, indicating his desire to pursue new avenues and to have the opportunity to make new major choices. Together with the Wheel in the central position and the other cards present in the Life Spread I feel this will bring positive changes.

Reid identifies with the Fool card as his desire to focus upon his writing, which would be an entirely new path for him to follow. Based on the cards in the work area and other indications, I feel this will have a positive outcome, although Death and the Tower may represent some major changes to deal with along the way. Reid's desires are strongly driven by the Fool; the Wheel is on his side, as is the World—all are powerful cards working in his favour!

The Anchor
IMMEDIATE FUTURE: THE TOWER
The Life Spread
FUTURE: THE QUEEN OF CUPS, FIVE OF SWORDS,
THE HERMIT, FOUR OF CUPS

It may be possible the Tower relates to a forthcoming situation, which appears to involve a Queen of Cups accompanied by the Five of Swords. This may not have any bearing on the Death card showing in the career section of the Anchor, however, and could be an entirely separate incident.

I do not feel the Queen of Cups is related to the situation shown in the love area, as this is moving towards good news and possible stability in the future. Neither does she seem to be connected to the particular situation shown in the work area of the Life Spread, since they are also positive. This tends to isolate the situation but as these cards are in the future position of the Life Spread, and the Tower sits in the immediate future position, they could be connected.

The cards accompanying the Queen of Cups show she is not well-aspected. The Five of Swords usually shows someone with a hidden agenda who is not working for Reid's benefit; often this card represents deceit, dishonesty, or underhandedness. It can also show something lost by unfair means. The Hermit following shows that this will cause contemplation and perhaps withdrawal from the person or situation. As a card of wisdom, I think it shows he will become aware of whatever plot lies behind the Five of Swords, or it will cause him to consider the matter quite deeply. The Four of Cups suggests a sense of inner discontent with the outcome. The Four is not a particularly damaging card; instead, it represents more of a discontented emotional state, aversion, a further sign of withdrawal, and ultimately perhaps an outward air of indifference to the matter.

After informing Reid of what I see, I describe the Queen of Cups, so he could recognise her if already known, or when she makes an appearance. The Queen of Cups is usually quite gentle-natured and non-confrontational, empathic and sensitive, or indicates someone with artistic or creative leanings. In the negative, as shown here, they can be childish, clingy, self-centred, manipulative, or possibly prone to a victim mentality. It is possible she could represent a Water sign, although I normally avoid identifying people with astrological signs, as it is not something we always readily know. Personality traits and characteristics are therefore more reliable for recognition.

Reid cannot identify this person with anyone he knows at the moment, however I remind him that since she is in the future section of the reading it may be that he has not yet encountered her.

I am not fully convinced that the Tower is connected to these cards, as I would have expected them to reflect a stronger situation—it is possible it represents a completely separate incident. I explain the Tower's meaning to Reid but also tell him I feel quite frustrated because I do not feel I can confidently identify a situation to connect it to in order to advise him more fully. Given the cards in front of me, I explain that I feel the situation is either an isolated incident or one that he would overcome, although it may present some difficulty. Had the results been more far-reaching, I am sure the other cards would have reflected this.

Unlike the Death card, which in many ways Reid is aware of and actually aiming towards, I explain that the Tower usually brings finality to something he may not be expecting, so it can produce a few shockwaves. Often the Tower can clear away something from our life that we may have falsely believed to be true, so it can allow the opportunity to remove falsehood and start again from a better position—from this angle it is of course possible to associate it with the Five of Swords and Queen of Cups. However, I explain that unfortunately I do not feel there are sufficient indications in the other cards to be able to suggest where I think the external problem could arise. I tell Reid it is possible that if we address the cards with more specific questions, the situation may show more clearly.

The Anchor
FUTURE: THE HIGH PRIESTESS

My frustration as a reader is compounded with the High Priestess in the final position. With a Tower incident I cannot connect or expand upon and now a message of "secrets that will be to his benefit once known," I feel it is starting to sound a little bit cryptic or ambiguous on my part. Unfortunately, this is what the cards have provided me with so I know there is relevance to their presence, whether or not I can see it.

As the card that concludes the reading for future indications, the High Priestess read alone is a reminder for Reid to trust and listen to his instincts, intuition, or gut feelings. Whilst the future remains as yet unknown, she can bring information, secrets, or mysteries that will be revealed to him at just the right moment to aid on his journey. (Enlightening perspectives when faced with a card that is presently not ringing many bells for me!)

My mind is racing to the point that it goes blank and suddenly I realise I've been having an "ego moment"—the importance of being seen to get it right, or how I was being perceived, had suddenly overtaken the actual reading's importance. I was frustrated because I wanted to do the best job I could and the answers were evading me, but this led to me getting in my own way. The realisation in itself is freeing and almost immediately I feel myself relax. Sometimes it just takes a moment to detach ourselves from the reading, take a deep breath, and reexamine the possibilities. I start to work through everything calmly and methodically.

The High Priestess informs us of secrets becoming known and may link to the message shown in the Life Spread's future area. With the Hermit following the Five of Swords, I feel the High Priestess will lend her insight to ensure limited damage on Reid's behalf in whatever is developing, as the information that becomes known works to his benefit. As the Hermit and the High Priestess are both major arcana cards, there is a theme of inner wisdom.

The High Priestess can indicate potential recognised (but not yet fully expressed) and can signify the subconscious, imagination, and creativity. Just as the High Priestess withdraws into the mystery of silence, so too does a writer. This is not a card we would normally associate with commercial business activities, as it focuses upon the deeper aspects of life and the subconscious mind. Interestingly enough, Reid has always maintained that he draws inspiration from the energy of the land; his writing reveals one who is highly attuned from working closely with nature as he seeks to portray the raw power and rugged beauty of his surrounding landscape.

This is perhaps a clue I missed previously, taking my immediate interpretation from the card's secrecy aspect. Yet I am reminded, as a result of my friend Sheila doing my cards, that the High Priestess always arises when I am deeply involved in my writing. It was not an association I initially made but one that has proven accurate over the years. Perhaps it provides insight into a further leaning towards this activity in the future for Reid.

With so much change appearing to be on the horizon, perhaps the High Priestess in the final position is not really so surprising. Following the thread through the Anchor alone we have the balanced thoughts from Justice, reassessment of his love life through the Hanging Man, major career change signalled by Death, the Wheel bringing in a new chapter, the unexpected events of the Tower, and the Fool showing his desire to pursue new paths. Combined with messages from the Life Spread of what appears to be the sale of the home ranch, movement in his love life, a longed for ambition successfully realised in the work area—a future "as yet unknown" now sits alongside rather nicely. It would seem that Reid should be looking at a different picture altogether in the future and, as such, there is bound to be far more than can be revealed at the present time. So, having exhausted every possibility, there are many ways the High Priestess can be interpreted in the reading … maybe not quite so obscure after all!

This leaves me with only the Tower unaccounted for. If this card is not connected to the situation regarding the Queen of Cups, it must be an isolated incident or one that Reid will overcome without affecting other matters. Having covered this card previously, I hope I have at least in some way prepared him for the emergence of such an event but also focussed upon the reading's positive aspects too.

With the reading complete, Reid asks me to summarise various areas, which we go through together briefly. I leave the spread in place and ask if he has any further questions before gathering up the cards from the Life Spread to move on to the Celtic Cross.

Additional Spread: Celtic Cross

Reid has been writing a Western saga, an ambitious project of six books covering a span of two hundred years. It is a huge undertaking alongside his normal business dealings and his writing of a nonfiction book on ranching. Reid would like to know if the series would get published.

In the first position, the Eight of Cups shows abandonment of a situation he has walked away from through disappointment and disillusion, despite putting in a lot of effort he abandons it to pursue a new path. The Queen of Wands crossing this card tends to show that she has been connected to this situation in some way. The Queen of Wands is loyal and protective towards family; people characterized by this card are always busy with a number of projects on the go, but can have a tendency to take on too much. Although usually of a warm disposition, they can also have a fiery nature.

The Wheel of Fortune in the third position provides more history to the matter showing that Reid felt it held promise, representing the start of a whole new cycle. Given what we know from the main spread and how he views his writing as a potential change in career direction, this card seems to resonate. Note also the Nine of Pentacles across from the Wheel.

The more recent past, the Eight of Swords, represents a situation where he felt restricted or uncertain as how to proceed.

Reid agrees that the cards are very accurate in their description with regard to the past history of an earlier writing partnership that he felt became untenable and consequently ended. The Eight of Swords required clarity of thought in moving the project forward; at first he felt it needed a co-author but following further consideration, decided to tackle it alone.

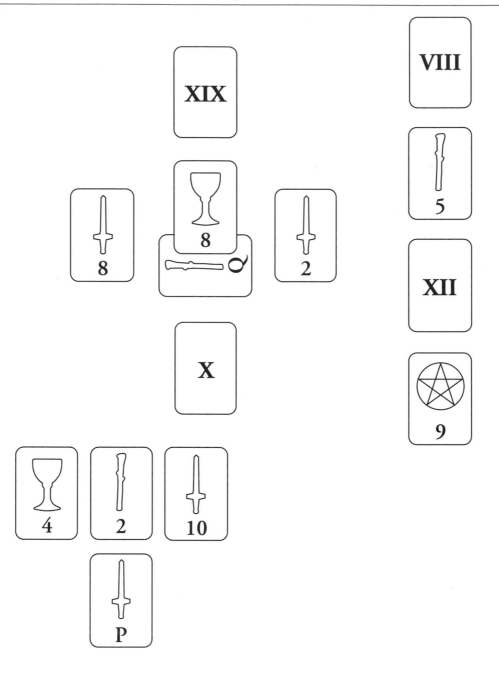

Note the Reader's Fan here, revealing more of the background already shown: the Four of Cups, the card of discontent; the Two of Wands for a partnership or collaboration; the Ten of Swords shows an ending; and the Page of Swords representing the delays.

The Sun in his crowning thoughts is the most positive card Reid could have, showing the strength of his ambition. As a card of shining success, it cannot be equalled. The Five of Wands is very revealing in the ninth position, balanced across from the Sun, showing petty obstacles and challenges. This not only connects to his experience so far but also hints that he may yet encounter a few more in the future. However, as the Sun is from the major arcana it has more power and influence, so the leaning will be towards this card rather than the Five of Wands from the minor arcana, so this should be easily overcome. The Nine of Pentacles is another good card, indicating pleasure and reward through one's own efforts, situated in the seventh position of apprehensions. With such positive cards located in the attitude areas is he in tune with the situation and where it ultimately leads? I believe so.

In the immediate future, the Two of Swords tends to indicate that a further deadlock or stalemate situation may be encountered, he may feel of two minds (literally, as the Two and with Swords representing the intellect) on how to proceed.

The Hanging Man in the eighth position perhaps provides more information here. As the card that shows how others will be viewing the situation, it indicates that he may still reassess the project further and could be viewing it from a different perspective in the future. It suggests that the books may undergo further reassessment of how he presents or writes them, or at least in the way he proceeds. Somehow it appears there will be a further change in the future. It could re-emphasise the meaning of the Two of Swords—a further period of suspension, which is not particularly the news Reid wants to hear, given the delays he has experienced so far. However, I feel that they are actions which are under his control—his thought processes and decisions on how to move forward.

I point out to Reid that there is the possibility that it could represent a publisher looking at his work but wanting him to present the books differently from how he had originally intended or envisioned. However, this would have been more pertinent had he asked about a specific publisher—as the eighth card would reveal how they were looking at the situation. Noting the way his question was phrased leaves it far more open as to how others will be looking in, per se. On that basis, my original interpretation would probably be stronger but I still feel it is an option worth mentioning, due to the question's openness. Publishers could be classified as the "others" looking in.

Strength in the final position shows that he will win through in the end, though it will require patience, diplomacy, quiet determination, inner strength, courage, and perseverance. With the driving force of the Sun in his crowning thoughts, we can see how relevant this card becomes towards manifesting his overall goal.

With the immediate future leading to the outcome, the Two of Swords will in some way bring about the success found in the Strength card, so once Reid moves forward from the situation found in the Two (providing he follows Strength's messages), he should succeed.

Results and Feedback

It was three months later when Reid and I finally caught up over his reading, with the usual reception problems of cell and satellite phone. Quite a lot had happened since the reading.

One Month Later

Reid was accepted into a mentoring programme for authors, which had involved submitting his work and securing a coveted place from many thousands of other hopeful applicants. The programme included personal mentoring with access to highly successful best-selling authors, editors, agents, and publicists, amongst others. As he didn't mentioned it previously, I was not aware Reid had applied—he informs me now that he had done so prior to the reading. (Ace of Pentacles with the three court cards, in the personal area of the Life Spread.)

We feel this also connects with the cards in the work area, which I had felt were connected to his writing rather than ranching business, due to the personal flavour of the cards here (Page of Wands, Temperance, Three of Cups, the World.)

Further developments on the writing front include a publisher looking at his ranching book, *Land for Love and Money*, with a further publisher and agent currently looking at the first completed book and forward proposal for the six-book series *Threads West: An American Saga.*

Within a month of the reading an offer was also received on a property connected to the home ranch, this deal wavered on and off over the last few months only to be replaced by new buyers entering the equation. These events tie in with the cards from the home area. With the Nine of Pentacles at the end of this group the outcome still appears hopeful.

Two Months Later

On the ranching business side of his life a major development project had to be significantly suddenly altered and, whilst still profitable, only represented a fraction of the original anticipated profits. Whilst it ties in with the Death card in the work area, I think this was the Tower, due to the nature of events. They were external forces over which Reid had no control that brought this about. He has the situation in hand so I am hopeful the Tower has now been experienced.

Three Months Later

Reid recently had his first radio interview with a large audience to promote his books. He has also launched the first book in the series from his website. As he states on his site, this is the attainment of a goal he set for himself forty-five years ago. This would certainly fit with the cards in the work area and most particularly the World. However, I think this is still a developing situation, so the best may yet be to come.

Given all that is happening here, it would seem that both the personal and work areas of Reid's Life Spread apply to his writing activities. With the Wheel of Fortune at the heart of the Anchor, many exciting opportunities are opening up for him.

Four Months Later

The book's launch went extremely well and exceeded his expectations. Reid is currently busy lining up further television and radio interviews to promote his ranching book.

Meanwhile, with his web designer, he seems to have hit onto something quite big connected to electronic publishing. From the description, it sounds like an exciting concept and I wonder if it connects to the Hanging Man and Two of Swords from his Celtic Cross, as it changes his goal plan slightly and the platform from which he presents his work. Being an innovative and successful businessman already, I comment that it appears difficult for Reid to just sit down and write a book without reinventing the publishing industry along the way!

The relationship cards remain an unspoken area, and one that Reid appears to be keeping close to his chest. However, he states that it relates to someone he has known for a number of years, and that is as much as he is prepared to reveal.

I ask if there have been any developments concerning the situation with the Queen of Cups. It appears this has now occurred, given his description. He was alerted to some spiteful comments brewing from a previous contact that were edging close to slander. Having given the matter some thought, he let it be known through mutual contacts that she would be wise to drop the matter before it gathered any more of his attention. He stated that he was too busy to become drawn into such petty issues and felt it just wasn't worth his time or energy. (Sounds like the Four of Cups.)

Five Months Later

Reid has been busy and tells me there have been some exciting developments regarding the publication of his books and some innovative marketing planned. This has involved a number of major decisions and various changes, including his forward plan of the presentation for the ranching book, *Land for Love and Money,* and partner workbook, *Green for Green.*

Meanwhile support for *Threads West* has been gathering momentum with some excellent endorsements and reviews from published authors and readers alike. Next month Karen Mayfield, best-selling author of *Wake Up Women: BE Happy, Healthy & Wealthy* and co-creator for the *Wake Up Women* book series, will be featuring his book on her website, which is big news indeed! Needless to say, Reid is delighted with the way things are progressing. From the cards in the Life Spread and Celtic Cross, it would seem he is well on his way now and we can see how the cards relate to what he is experiencing.

Six Months Later

On the first two days of its release, the launch of the paperback for *Threads West* achieved number one best-seller position in four different categories with Amazon, also number one Mover and Shaker (most active book) rising to number 173 on the overall sellers list and number 82 in hottest new releases. This was despite the book's site and orders with Amazon being down for nine hours, due to the volume of sales. The publisher and distributor took over to fulfil orders.

Just two weeks later, and now heading towards the seven-month mark since the original readings, the book garnered Best Western 2010 and runner-up Best Romance 2010 in the prestigious USA Book News awards for 2010. The relevance and results of the cards are now becoming more evident.

Reid's writing quest is no doubt part of a longer journey, but one in which we have been able to share the early stages of his success. If you would like to follow his continuing story you can find him at: www.ReidLRosenthal.com.

In Reid's Own Words

While I am a firm believer in energies, auras, and the power of old souls, and therefore believe in a greater current which can be tapped, felt, directed, I was admittedly a bit skeptical of Tarot. The translation of my spirituality, that connection between all things animate and inanimate, did not quite reach the point of believing in the cards being such a synapse. Josie's reading was interesting—no, make that fascinating. I learned much, and she was open with information about what each card signified, and how the combination of cards foretold a story. It was not until the periodic monthly updates, however, that the significance of the cards' power became apparent. Am I a believer in Tarot now? Almost. But my instinctive trust in the Force, that universal energy that permeates and surrounds us, has been made stronger than ever.

Reader's Tips
Telephone Readings

If you have never attempted a telephone reading before, the format is similar to the person being present, with the exception that you handle the cards on their behalf. You may wish to try this with your friends first to build some confidence, before offering to read for strangers.

Follow your usual format with reading cloth and decks in front of you, taking a few minutes to wind down and empty your mind beforehand. If I have a photograph of the person concerned I like to bring it up on the computer screen, as I feel that together with the sound of their voice it helps me tune into them, but I often work without photographs; they are my personal preference, if available.

Once you are on the line, explain the format the reading will take, and then ask the seeker to focus upon you shuffling the cards, which they can usually hear. Ask them to allow a reasonable time for you to shuffle (otherwise most tend to stop you too quickly) but when the moment feels right to let you know when to stop. Cut and lay out the cards.

As Internet and communication technology advances it is possible to telephone people free or with lower charges, even internationally, through various programs, applications, and software. Research the best option for you on the Internet.

If you prefer to use landline phone services, consider whether you call the seeker or they call you. I was surprised by how many people automatically assumed my number would be the premium rate variety with expensive per-minute charges. Over time as you get busier, you could also find yourself bombarded by calls without appointments once they have your number, or those who forget the international time difference and call in the middle of the night.

In the early stages the luxury of a separate line purely for your readings is probably far from your mind, so the Internet option does provide some good benefits. If you use a landline phone it is usually preferable for you to call the seeker and allow the cost of the call in your charge for the reading…just remember to calculate and confirm the time zone differences!

9
The Mad Hatter

Michael Harrison is the founder of the Mad Hatter Tea Company from Richmond, in North Yorkshire, so named because Lewis Carroll attended school in Richmond. As fate would have it our appointment was scheduled for April 1st—very fitting for the Mad Hatter but not an April Fools' prank, we assure you. Michael is in his late forties and married, with four adult children.

I have never read for Michael before but the Tarot is no stranger to him, although he informs me his Thoth deck has not been used for many years now. He feels very comfortable about having a reading and is looking forward to it. Even though Tarot is familiar territory to him, I still cover the same information as I do for everyone, as not all Tarot readers work to the same format.

First Impressions

- With the High Priestess, Devil, and Moon in the Anchor there appears to be a good deal of secrecy and unknown facts yet to emerge, possibly connected to the work area.

- The Tower in the wishes section of the Anchor reveals a desire for complete change.

- The first (top) three quadrants of the Life Spread and the last (bottom) two seem to be divided by an invisible line, as if focussed on two completely different things.

- The amount and type of Sword cards in the Life Spread in the first three quadrants appear to show considerable stress.

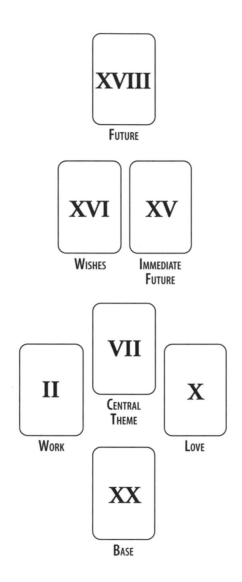

The Mad Hatter—Life Spread

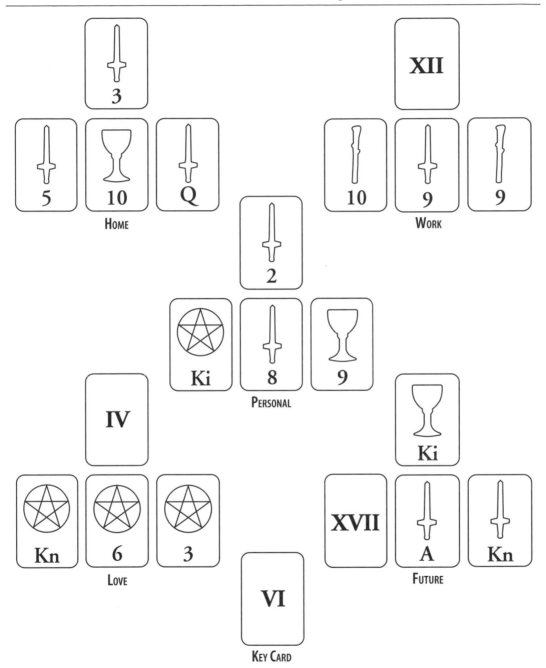

The Anchor
BASE POSITION: JUDGEMENT

Starting with Judgement in the first position of the Anchor I ask Michael if there has been a revival or renewal around him recently—the card suggests he is currently dealing with something that has roots in the past but represents a new beginning. Michael tells me that he started to develop Mad Hatter Tea about ten years ago, but in recent months has thrown himself into working for the company full-time. Sadly, he was in a position earlier of needing to relinquish the original parent food company, which took up most of his time before. Whilst he had always recognised the potential of Mad Hatter Tea it had been a slow process developing the blend in India and then making the necessary arrangements in England. Meanwhile, the parent company had always been very busy and demanded his full attention.

I tell Michael I find this very interesting, as Judgement is a karmic card and often represents a new beginning where lessons from the past have been learned. He can move on more positively, free from the restraints of things that may have held him back. As an added bonus, he is also wiser and more knowledgeable due to his experiences. He says this is certainly true but it has been a trying time.

The Anchor
WORK AREA: THE HIGH PRIESTESS
CENTRAL THEME: THE CHARIOT

It feels relevant to move across to the work area of the Anchor. The High Priestess represents information that is not yet known but once revealed will be to his benefit. I explain that there could be aspects of secrecy with this card although not usually in a negative way. Michael says that much is still unknown but he certainly hopes things will become more positive. I find his wording intriguing but move on to the central card, the Chariot, a card that suggests he is and will be working hard in the near future. However, if he can maintain his workload, he should overcome any obstacles. Michael says this is very good news.

The Life Spread
Personal Area: Two of Swords, King of Pentacles, Eight of Swords, Nine of Cups

The Two of Swords is the very first card of the Life Spread, so I ask Michael if he currently feels in a deadlock situation in some way. The King of Pentacles is followed by the Eight of Swords so I say that the deadlock may revolve around a man connected to finances or a successful businessman. Here Michael's story takes on a deeper relevance and suggestions of the "stress" cards becomes evident. He tells me there is someone who would fit the description of the King of Pentacles, whom he feels caused considerable anxiety and bad feelings within his family. In addition, there are a number of financial people involved in wrapping up the affairs of the original company and until they get back to him he doesn't know what his own position will be, or how bad things could get. Michael is smiling and positive in his manner but he constantly rubs his fingers across his forehead, revealing underlying stress and worries. I have already assimilated the cards in the work area in relation to what he is saying, all the pieces fit together, with the relevance of the Eight of Swords in the personal area and the Nine of Swords in the work area underlining his emotional state and their reason for being.

I tell him there are some good indications in the reading that improve as it progresses, which I will cover as we go. Firstly, I am pleased to say that the personal situation concerning his finances should have a favourable outcome. With the "wish" card (the Nine of Cups) at the end of this situation, the suggestion is that the future holds a positive outcome he will be happy with. This could equally apply to the other person he mentioned. However, taking into account all the other cards in front of us, none of the cards we would expect to see representing hardship and loss appear to be on the horizon. Michael says this is very good news!

Were we looking at more dire results, such as Michael fears, I would expect to see cards such as the Five of Pentacles, Ten of Swords, Death, or the Tower in the future positions. The company's affairs have not yet been finalised, which may also explain why none of these cards are showing in past positions, even though these events have happened only in the last few months.

The Life Spread
Work Area: The Hanging Man, Ten of Wands, Nine of Swords, Nine of Wands
The Anchor
Central Area: The Chariot
Wishes Area: The Tower

I explain that the cards in the work area reveal a similar theme to Michael's personal area, which is not unusual, given the situation he has described and how most of his attention in his life relates to this presently.

The Hanging Man is similar to the Two of Swords in that it shows how he may be feeling that life is currently in suspension. Michael interjects that things are difficult since the outcome could affect his future business activities and way of life substantially; he just wants to get on with everything now but feels unable to do so until the old company's affairs are finalized. I remark that the Tower in the wishes position of the Anchor clearly reflects this desire.

However, moving back to the Hanging Man I also cover the more positive side, revealing that he has taken a step back and reassessed matters. He is now looking at things from a different perspective in order to gain a better understanding of his position. This card also speaks of sacrifices being made in the shorter term in the interest of gaining something of greater benefit in the future. In Michael's case, the sacrifice appears to have been the painful decision of relinquishing the old company which has enabled him to focus upon the new path before him.

The Ten of Wands shows the burden he felt he was carrying with the Nine of Swords—the worries that surrounded him. With the Nine of Swords in the central position and the Eight of Swords in the central position of his personal area, I explain that he may have a little ways to go before these feelings are behind him. However, there is light ahead on his road. The Nine of Wands informs him not to give up no matter how weary he may feel, for often this card represents the final hurdle that must be overcome in order to attain an objective. This card is much like turning the corner, if he can just gather together all his reserves for that final push.

In many respects, the Nine of Wands and the Chariot reinforce each other with a repeated message: it will take courage and determination on Michael's part, but he can win through with persistence. As the Chariot is the central card of the Anchor this tends to magnify the message. It could be a bumpy road but one he can traverse through safely if he takes the right approach and can stay focussed on the goal ahead. With three nines in the mix, the penultimate numbered cards of the minor arcana, it appears to accentuate the message of being close to completion. Michael says this is a relief to hear and smiles broadly when I tell him that the best of the reading is still to come.

The Life Spread
HOME AREA: THREE OF SWORDS, FIVE OF SWORDS, TEN OF CUPS, QUEEN OF SWORDS
KEY CARD: THE LOVERS
The Anchor
RELATIONSHIP AREA: THE WHEEL OF FORTUNE

These cards appear to be a curious mix at first glance; I tell Michael that the appearance of the Three and Five of Swords suggests there may have been a quarrel that has affected the family or some sort of division. The Five indicates there may be a sense of injustice, underhanded secrecy, or unfairness at play, as this card often shows people with a hidden agenda, or things taken in a selfish or unfair manner without regard for others. (We have seen from previous case studies the different types of activities this card can imply.) Yet next to it we have the Ten of Cups, representing happiness and contentment, followed by a Queen of Swords, a lady I would describe as possessing great inner strength.

Michael immediately identifies this card with his wife and explains that they have always had a close relationship that provides stability and support to both, but life has become difficult for the family since the situation surrounding the Three and Five of Swords had occurred. He tells me the description of the two cards is very accurate and relates to a hurtful situation connected to work and the King of Pentacles. He hopes the situation is one the family can work through in time. "Importantly," he informs me, "we just want to move on now, as there's nothing to be gained by dwelling on the past." How very wise!

Given the situation as Michael has explained it, it could be that this set of cards connect and read together as a group. Since the Queen of Swords is in the final placement of this area, it could also show that the future will depend on her actions in some way. Michael informs me that his wife was also involved with the parent company, which may explain the importance of the Lovers as the Key card.

The Wheel of Fortune in the Anchor shows that luck is on his side with a new cycle commencing. There should be some positive indications in his life, heading in a more favourable direction in the near future.

The Life Spread
Relationship Area: The Emperor, Knight of Pentacles, Six of Pentacles, Three of Pentacles

From my initial impressions, it was the last two quadrants of the spread that gave the appearance of the reading having an invisible line drawn horizontally across the centre. The entirety of Michael's reading has so far focussed upon work—given his situation, it is perhaps no surprise that work continues to feature.

I tell Michael that this is where the reading takes a definite positive turn; in many ways I feel we are following a continuous strand as the reading progresses, weaving into future.

The Emperor as the Key card of the area is excellent for work issues. It shows leadership, ambition, authority, and the strength to make things happen. Logic and rationality have been applied, and the Knight of Pentacles shows the eventual fruition of something that appears to have dragged on for a long time, so far without many results despite methodical and persistent effort. Michael says he feels sure this must be the tea company. Although it had been showing some promise, he now has more time he can fully invest, and the company is beginning to deliver results.

I explain my thoughts to Michael about how I feel his reading is divided into two parts, with the upper section focussing upon the recent events of the old company and the bottom section completely upon the tea company, which is now his main and future focus. I tell him that whilst things were difficult after all the personal and financial investment in the original company, he never would have had the time to truly concentrate on the tea company—not while the parent company demanded his time. Michael said this was true and he had never considered it in this way before.

The Six of Pentacles suggests financial increase with generosity, gifts, and sharing as its theme, so finances will start to improve. The Three of Pentacles shows work that he enjoys and has natural talent and ability for will start bringing him recognition. Aside from the trials and tribulations of the existing situation, Michael tells me he finds the Mad Hatter concept very exciting and the feedback from visitors to the website has been excellent.

The Life Spread
FUTURE AREA: KING OF CUPS, THE STAR,
ACE OF SWORDS, KNIGHT OF SWORDS

I smile as I tell Michael that the cards continue to show improvement. The Star is a perfect card to be found here and I am so pleased to be able to relay it, as it is everything I could hope to convey to him in his current position. Assuring and promising better times ahead, the Star informs him to have faith, optimism, and hope for the future.

The Ace of Swords alongside brings additional power to the situation, the one I always consider as the "ace up the sleeve," as it carries a great deal of support for the seeker. No matter what life throws into the mix, they will always win out in the end with this card on their side. Strength and triumph over adversity are key indicators with the Ace of Swords and, with the Knight of Swords following, I would suggest that once events turn they would do so at a rapid rate, as this Knight brings considerable speed into the equation. I tell him to be sure to be ready, for when things take off it could feel quite manic. Michael appears considerably happier than when we first began and is thoroughly delighted by this news.

I point to the King of Cups, relating to this character's easygoing nature. Michael feels sure this is an old friend who has been very helpful to and supportive of him through the difficult period. As the King is in the future position I advise that Michael may not know him yet but he certainly has a bearing on the future cards. Since the King of Cups can be a creative type and he sits just before the Star, I laugh and say that it would be nice if it were Johnny Depp! Michael assures me that he intends to send him a complimentary box of Mad Hatter Tea and we both laugh heartily. Joking aside, I tell Michael that the recent launch of the new *Alice in Wonderland* film, starring Johnny Depp, is an incredible stroke of luck of timing that surely could not fail to create a welcome boost of interest for the Mad Hatter Tea Company.

The Anchor
IMMEDIATE FUTURE: THE DEVIL
FUTURE: THE MOON

I have purposely left these two cards for last, as Michael's reading had enough stress factor in the early section. With so many positive indications in the future, I did not wish to dampen the mood. I feel there is a connection with the High Priestess here in the work area and with the three cards together, my real feeling is that there are elements of secrecy that have yet to be revealed, but will be to Michael's benefit once they are. There is nothing further that we can say here and, as with most stories and circumstances, there is often more going on under the surface than we can see, as the Moon clearly tells us. However, with this card in the final position I am sure that the facts of the situation will be revealed in the fullness of time.

In summary, I remind Michael that whilst there appears to be a short period where the current circumstances of feeling weighed down and worried will still be with him, the future shows his situation will start to clear. He needs to remain focussed and single-minded upon his path, and continue to work hard and remain positive—circumstances will begin to change and gather momentum. Whilst the results of the reading could take up to a year to fully manifest they should begin to change within a matter of months.

Michael tells me that he found the reading very enlightening and that he feels much happier and relieved at what the cards show.

I ask Michael if there is anything further he would like to know. He tells me there is only one question he would like to ask, "What is the future of the Mad Hatter Tea Company?" I gather the cards up from the Life Spread and hand them back to Michael to shuffle, asking him to focus upon his question as he does so.

Additional Spread: Celtic Cross

The four tens are hard to miss; as the final numbered card in the minors they represent a completion and transitional period from one phase of life to another. All four being present indicates it would be true about life across the board. Given Michael's story, it is interesting to see it reflected before us.

The Ten of Cups presently surrounding him suggests the importance of the relationship connected to the work situation. As the Ten of Wands is the history behind the first card it shows the feelings of overburden from the old company affairs and the effect this has had on the present position. Note how the King of Pentacles is balanced across from the Ten of Wands, the source of Michael's worry and "burdens." However, the Three of Pentacles as the crossing card is favourable, relating to the work being done with the new company.

As the most recent past, the Page of Swords can represent delays or disappointing news, or possible trouble with a child. The two tens balanced across from one another in the crowning thoughts (position 5) and hopes (position 9) remind us of the fears Michael spoke of earlier, the stability of their family home. Read separately, however, the Ten of Pentacles is his crowning thoughts—a good, strong, positive card in tune with what he is trying to achieve.

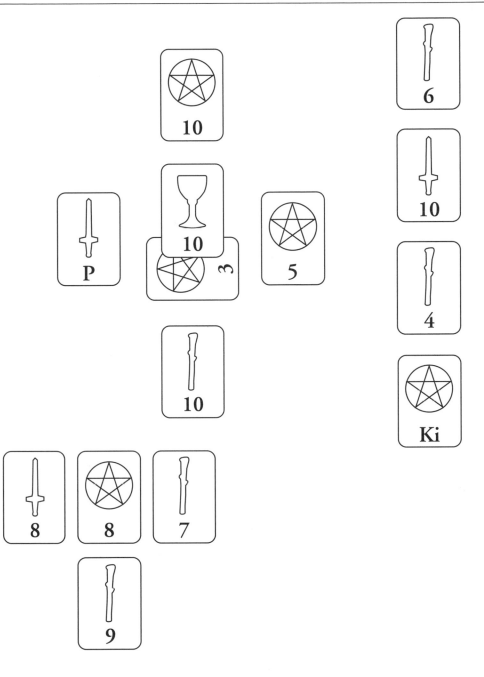

So far, I feel the cards are a good reflection of the situation we have discussed from his main reading and, whilst the Five of Pentacles shows us that things may be a little tough financially in the immediate future, there are good longer-term indications. The Six of Wands as the bearer of great news should bring victory, rewards, achievement, and recognition. The Four of Wands in position 8 means that others will be viewing his situation as one of stability. Michael is delighted and tells me this is very encouraging.

The Reader's Fan as the background information is quite clear, providing a recap of the original main reading. Now that we know the circumstances of Michael's life, we can see how well these fit into place. The worries of the Eight of Swords, the new work of the apprentice in the Eight of Pentacles, the Seven of Wands representing his courage to stand up for the beliefs and ideals of things that are important to him, and the required determination of the Nine of Wands to fight through challenging times.

Michael tells me he has really enjoyed the reading, then with suitable Mad Hatter flourish produces his tea, takes over my kitchen, and presents a rather wonderful cuppa. "In celebration," he says, "of a very happy un-birthday." I'll drink to that!

Results and Feedback

Four Months Later

This has been the first time Michael and I have had the opportunity to meet up since his reading. However, the timing of our catch-up is rather good, since most of his results have come around just recently.

Michael appears much happier and relaxed than when I last saw him and he reports that things are starting to look promising. He has been beavering away, promoting the company and attending meetings with potential commercial customers. The Mad Hatter brand is proving phenomenally popular with the public, attracting a large following and customer base from around the world to the website and online shop.

Aside from independent and specialist traders, he has started to make inroads with a well-known upmarket department chain store, and also the National Trust (which supports historic buildings open to the public in the UK), railway, and airline companies. As a result of ongoing meetings, he is feeling particularly pleased that his company has now secured a large contract with a railway network just a few days ago. This has resulted in some fairly urgent activity on their behalf, since the order will require specialist branded cups and associated products. Michael reports that everything is in hand, tea production on a larger scale had already been anticipated, and it has been very exciting. He has even had an inquiry from a trading company in China that loved the Mad Hatter concept. It throws a whole new light on the saying "selling tea to China"—quite an accolade!

These events certainly tie in with the future area of his Life Spread reading. When asked about the King of Cups, he informs me that his friend invested into the company and became a shareholder, which has been enormously helpful. This would seem to also reflect the Six of Pentacles in the love area. Overall, things are starting to take off.

Michael tells me it has been a tough time but the future seems promising now and he is really enjoying the work, which he finds personally exciting, as there are so many associated product areas they plan to expand upon with the concept.

When I ask him about the situation with the King of Pentacles, he explains that the affairs of the old company still have not been finalised and he isn't too sure when he would hear, although he believes it won't be much longer. The other King of Pentacles (that he had mentioned and connected the card to) had appeared at his home, resulting in some air being cleared between the two. It would seem that the High Priestess, Devil, and Moon were accurate in this regard, with some light being shed on various issues. Michael felt happy that he could close the door and walk away from the past now, very firmly focussed on the future.

Five Months Later

Michael has secured more large contracts for the company; things are really gathering steam. In addition, he has just received some very good news from the King of Pentacles, who was wrapping up the affairs of the old company—so it seemed this court card proved accurate to both people and situations to which it was connected. Finances have improved and the future suddenly looks a lot brighter than it did at our first reading.

I am delighted to hear how well things are going and notice quite the difference in Michael since I last saw him. I am sure we will be hearing more about the Mad Hatter Tea Company in the future. You can follow the rest of his and the company's story as it progresses and join in the fun at their website: www.madhattertea.co.uk.

In Michael's Own Words

At the time of my reading, I had just had my fingers burnt in a business deal, having made my fortune and lost it. Very careless! I blamed myself for not realising my trust had been misplaced. Having lost the company I had built from scratch over twenty years, I felt I was in the midst of chaos.

Josie told me that there was hope and bright prospects on the horizon, but I wasn't too sure! She also made some accurate predictions concerning my former company.

But the previous year's entire turnover was eclipsed in the first three months of this year's trading. As a standalone company and without the constraints of carrying deadwood, I was back, but to build a business from the beginning again. I needed premises, a vehicle, an office, etc. I went to see an old friend and we agreed on a plan to move forward. Having the time to fully concentrate on the Mad Hatter now, everything started to take off almost immediately.

I threw myself into Mad Hatter Tea and right now am working on a voluntary basis. This is a natural business decision, but within the next three to four months, I will be earning as much as I did before the crash of my former company. To do this in such a short time is nothing less than a miracle! I have not been as happy in my work as I am now for years.

As of press time, we currently supply some national up-market accounts with another about to come on stream this month. With numerous farm shops and delicatessens nationally, we also supply to castles, tourist destinations, and the National Trust. Our website has become very popular, with many international visitors. In addition, we have just been enlisted to supply a major railway company that will in effect more than triple our existing turnover.

From my reading with Josie the cards told all that I have written here. My confidence has returned, and I believe that confidence is based on the ethical building block of success. I am beginning to believe she is right and aim for a positive outcome. Wish us luck!

Reader's Tips
Multiple Numbered Cards

Multiple cards that share the same number can provide another layer of information outside of their individual interpretation. If you follow numerology, astrology, or elemental associations, you can apply these on top of the original spread for further information. You might also have your own interpretations you could apply.

You may wish to consider the importance of multiple numbers if there are three or four of the same number present. Even if you do not apply all the multiple numbers to your readings I have found the indicators that can be most helpful are: Aces, Fives, Sevens, Tens, Kings, and Queens.

Here is a list of meanings I currently consider in my own readings when they appear in multiples. The main ones are highlighted in bold text.

- **Aces—beginnings and a period of exciting new starts.**
- Twos—continuation, unity, partnership, balance.
- Threes—initial progress, expansion, growth.
- Fours—structure and stability.
- **Fives—challenges and instability.**
- Sixes—harmony and improvement.
- **Sevens—a changing phase.**
- Eights—number of infinity; flow and movement.
- Nines—penultimate, "almost there," preparation, and tying up loose ends.
- **Tens—transition to completion.**
- Pages—external messages are significant.
- Knights—energy and action.
- **Kings and Queens—indicates a number of other people involved.**

10
The Yoga Teacher

$\mathcal{J}$acquelyn Berry is a yoga teacher who runs a website that organises stress management and well-being workshops throughout the United Kingdom. Her clients have ranged from prisoners to celebrity sportspeople and everyone in between. She is in her mid-forties, divorced, with one child.

I have never read for Jacquelyn before, although she informs me she has previously had a Tarot reading and found it helpful at the time.

First Impressions

- The amount of court cards in the work area of the Life Spread.

- Repeat of the Star in the Anchor and Life Spread.

- Repeat of Strength in the Anchor and Life Spread.

- Three fours later in the reading, perhaps leading to greater stability.

From the starting position of the Anchor I ask Jacquelyn if she has recently been going through a period of soul-searching or deep thought. The Hermit suggests contemplation or the need to withdraw in order to find quiet space to access answers regarding life issues. Jacquelyn says this would be true and she has recently been doing a lot of meditation. I tell her I cannot think of a better card to reflect this, since the Hermit's message tells us we have all the answers we need within ourselves—we just need the quiet time to tune into them.

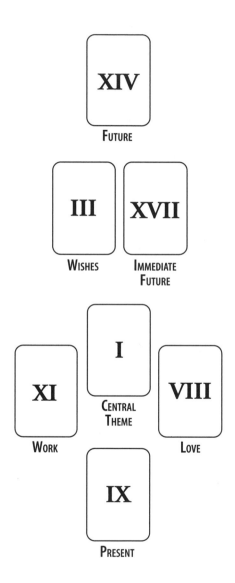

The Yoga Teacher—Life Spread

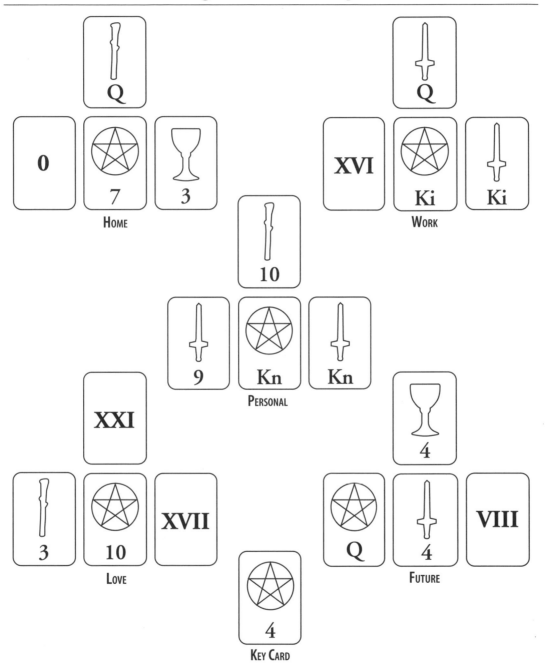

The Life Spread
PERSONAL AREA: TEN OF WANDS, NINE OF SWORDS, KNIGHT OF PENTACLES, KNIGHT OF SWORDS

Moving straight across to the personal area of the Life Spread, we see the Ten of Wands in the first position. I ask Jacquelyn if she has been feeling overburdened with work or life in general—if there is anything else that may be causing her to feel this way. Jacquelyn agrees so I continue with the Nine of Swords and ask if she has been worrying about this in some way. She says it is nothing in particular, rather things in general.

As I can see what the cards are indicating in the future of this situation I want to define it more clearly, to avoid her attaching it to something that may not be correct. Aside from the Tower in the work area (which has caught my attention but may not have been experienced yet) I can see nothing else reflecting this situation elsewhere in the spread. We are also right at the beginning of the reading—the cards we have could relate to any area of life, so I take time to try and pinpoint it with her.

I explain to Jacquelyn the cards show that she has been feeling bogged down in some way and worrying about it and, because it falls into her personal area, it must be pertinent in some way and affecting her on a personal level. With the Knight of Pentacles following, I explain that I believe this is regarding something that has been ongoing or that she has been working towards for quite some time but has not yet seen the full results. Jacquelyn says she feels this is work related in connection with some workshops she has been trying to establish and a workbook she has been developing over the last two years.

I tell Jacquelyn that the Knight of Pentacles informs us that a situation she has been methodically and diligently working towards but as yet seen no results will finally be forthcoming. In addition, the Knight of Swords brings a swift moving energy into play, so when things do take off, they should happen fairly quickly. Two knights together also shows a great deal of energy around the situation. So although she may have been preparing for some time, I tell her that she needs to ensure she is ready to go with everything once it takes off, as she could otherwise be caught out by the speed of events.

The Anchor
WORK AREA: JUSTICE
The Life Spread
WORK AREA: QUEEN OF SWORDS, THE TOWER,
KING OF PENTACLES, KING OF SWORDS
The Anchor
CENTRAL THEME: THE MAGICIAN

Following the natural flow the reading is taking, I move across to the work areas. Justice is showing balanced thought being applied to matters with the possibility of contracts and agreements, so I ask if she has any contracts around her at the moment in relation to work. Jacquelyn says she doesn't at the moment. I explain that with Justice appearing, she will need to take a logical viewpoint regarding work matters and that contracts may feature in future dealings in this area.

The work area of the Life Spread is full of people and aside from the Tower, there is no other action being shown, so the people indicated in the court cards should feature quite strongly. As it is the Key card, my immediate thought is that the influence of the Queen of Swords should have already been felt, possibly in connection with the Tower. The following two kings are moving away from the situation the Tower brought, so they may be unrelated or separate. This will reply upon whether Jacquelyn has experienced the Tower yet and how it relates to everything, or if it is still yet to come. Being the first card of the trio, it is most likely to have been felt already, although as we have seen from some of the other case studies this is not always so. I tell Jacquelyn that there appears to be a lot of people involved, although I am not being shown particular events. Whether or not she knows them all yet they will in some way feature quite strongly.

The central card of the reading is a clue I should have seen straight away but whose relevance is only clear to me now as I work through the reading. The Magician is usually connected to work matters and as it holds the central position, is the central theme of the Anchor. As obvious as this may sound, it is something that is becoming clearer to me through having to chart and follow up each of the case studies.

I am explaining the relevance of the Magician card to Jacquelyn (perhaps inwardly softening the blow of having to approach the Tower next!). An excellent card for the central position, the Magician shows she has all the skills and ability she needs to handle a task well and bring it to a successful conclusion. In order to do so requires her to take action and initiative, apply concentration and willpower, and have confidence in her own ability. As she is suitably pleased with this card's message, I next move on to tackle the work area of the Life Spread.

I describe the Queen of Swords as a lady of considerably strong character and a forthright manner. She is someone who is not afraid to speak out and is in some way connected or featuring in Jacquelyn's work area quite prominently. Jacquelyn says she can identify with these statements. I ask if something has come to an end recently, something that she wasn't expecting, that may have come as a bit of a shock, possibly connected to this lady. She tells me of two separate situations that happened recently with two different ladies, and both fit the description of the Queen of Swords. In both instances, the turn of events had surprised her and brought an end to her plans of potentially involving them in future business activities. I feel relieved that the Tower has already passed.

With the King of Pentacles and King of Swords moving into the future I tell Jacquelyn that these two men will in some way be important to her business dealings. Although we do not have any "action" cards in this area, there appear to be enough indications in the rest of the spreads to show that all should be well and, with the Magician in the centre and moving to the Star in the Anchor, I feel they will be beneficial to her.

I describe the King of Pentacles as a man who may be a successful businessman, either financially successful or possibly connected to finance; they can also be landowners and people who take a steady and methodical approach in their dealings. The King of Swords may be connected to uniforms, law, or government. As a personality type they have very agile minds, or can appear quite serious. These descriptions do not mean anything to Jacquelyn at the moment, so I tell her that if she hasn't met them yet, they are to make an entrance and will prove to be quite important to her in relation to her work and business.

The Life Spread
HOME AREA: QUEEN OF WANDS, THE FOOL, SEVEN OF PENTACLES, THREE OF CUPS

Another court card appears as the Key card of the home area. I describe the Queen of Wands as a warm and cheerful lady, who is usually very busy with plenty on the go. Queen of Wands types tend to be quite practical and homely people and whereas the Queen of Cups would spend hours listening to your problems, the Queen of Wand's way of helping would be to try and *do* something for you instead, which is one of the reasons she sometimes ends up taking on too much. Jacquelyn cannot readily associate anyone with this card in her home area.

I explain that sometimes when someone has an overriding theme in his or her life, it will reflect in other areas of the spread and, since she sometimes works from home, it could still be connected to work issues.

I then move on to the Fool and ask if there has been a recent, completely new and unexpected situation that may connect to the Queen of Wands. Jacquelyn says there has been a situation exactly as described, completely out of the blue and connected to a lady of this description, leading to a potentially new and exciting work opportunity. (Bingo!) With the Seven of Pentacles and Three of Cups following I tell her that this looks set to proceed and should create cause for celebration. The Seven of Pentacles represents gathering in her metaphorical harvest and can show the culmination of things coming to fruition in a way that will be financially beneficial to her. The Three of Cups tells of abundance, growth, emotional happiness, and cause for celebration.

The Anchor
Love Area: Strength
Immediate Future: The Star
Hopes and Wishes: The Empress
The Life Spread
Love Area: The World, Three of Wands, Ten of Pentacles, The Star

Strength in the love area of the Anchor is a particularly powerful card for women as it provides a certain kind of magnetism. The feminine qualities of patience, diplomacy, and inner strength are suggested here as a way of achieving aims as against more aggressive, male tendencies; "feminine charms" comes to mind. Jacquelyn smiles as she tells me she is not in a relationship but the first part appears accurate as she has been receiving quite a lot of offers recently. I tell her that perhaps the message of patience is important here and if she continues to receive this type of attention the right one may appear, given time. Strength is a good card for attraction.

In the love area of the Life Spread, the World as the Key card represents triumphant achievement and successful conclusion. With the Three of Wands in the first position, and the cards that follow, I feel that this further relates to business activities. Jacquelyn cannot associate with these cards at the moment. We explore various possibilities she suggests but they do not fit the scale of the World or the relevance of the Three of Wands. After I describe the cards for her, she concedes that they do not fit to anything presently around her. I explain that if this is the case, the cards provide an exciting glimpse of the potential that lies ahead.

The Three of Wands shows initial progress being made with business activities; this would be sufficient for her to feel pleased with her efforts but to also continue making plans for the future, building upon the first stages of success. The Ten of Pentacles represents enjoying comfort and security and points to financial increase. The home and family is also an important aspect of this card, often representing the family home in some way and with stability. The Star concluding the sequence brings the message of having optimism and faith in the future, as a card of hope it is the guiding light on the horizon, promising and assuring of better times ahead. This card has a gentle healing quality and may also suggest public recognition; both would be relevant in Jacquelyn's work and what she is trying to achieve. I point out that she also has the Star in the immediate future of the Anchor.

A further interesting aspect is that Jacquelyn reveals she has previously travelled quite extensively with her work, including internationally (on some levels the World would tie into this, although normally I consider it a lesser meaning unless it appears with other travel cards to strengthen the message.) Her work has never been centred on her home area, whereas at the moment she is working here. I explain that I believe the Ten of Pentacles represents her home's stability and with the other cards, I feel she should concentrate on making this her base and central point of her activities, because it would appear this is where the success generates. Jacquelyn says she would also feel happier about this because of her daughter.

The Star is an interesting card for someone who has worked with celebrities and high profile clients. More recently, Jacquelyn has worked with a number of premiere league footballers in England, so perhaps more of this will follow. The World and the Star together are excellent indicators for public recognition and a high profile.

Since the World as the Key card is not being experienced at the moment, I feel it pulls the other three together, since the Key card is the "atmosphere" or consolidation card of the area, representing the culmination of triumphant achievement for the things she is working towards.

As these cards appear in the love area, I feel that whilst work is the important theme, it also leads to stability in the home life found in the Ten of Pentacles, particularly with the Star as the final card. For the moment, she may need to focus on securing her career position and working towards the success of her business, but I believe that love will find her in the process. The Star and the World in the love area are two of the most positive in the Tarot, and the World tells of personal success on many levels. It may not be immediate, but I feel it could also point to the way in which love will enter her life.

As we note, there is no Ace of Cups or other relationship cards indicated in the spreads as such, but this does not mean her life will be devoid of relationships—they are just not the main focus at the moment. However, with cards such as Strength, the Ten of Pentacles, the Star, *and* the World all appearing in love areas, I am sure love will be on the horizon at some stage in the near future.

Moving to the hopes and wishes section of the Anchor, I note the Empress and ask if a serious loving relationship or marriage is something she strongly desires. Jacquelyn says yes but also that it must be with the right man, whom she feels she hasn't met yet. Since it is also the card of motherhood, it could reflect desires she has about her relationship with her daughter and how important she is to her. Jacquelyn feels this is especially true as a lone parent.

The Life Spread
FUTURE AREA: FOUR OF CUPS, QUEEN OF PENTACLES, FOUR OF SWORDS, STRENGTH
The Life Spread
KEY CARD: FOUR OF PENTACLES

Upon first appearance the final cards may seem anticlimatic following such exciting indications. The Four of Cups can show withdrawal due to a lack of interest or enthusiasm and can sometimes warn against not missing an opportunity due to this mood. As it leads the trio, the Queen of Pentacles appears important here; she could be a successful businesswoman, property or landowner, and/or wealthy; alternatively it tells of a possible connection to finance or earthy vocations in some way. Personality-wise, she is usually methodical in her dealings, organised, practical, and down to earth. Jacquelyn knows two people who fit this description. However, as the card is the future area, I explain it is quite possible she hasn't met this person yet.

I feel there are a couple of possibilities in this area; with the Four of Swords following, they could be telling of withdrawal, as this card can symbolise an inactive period, a time for rest and recovery to recharge one's batteries, or time to regather resources before moving forwards. The withdrawal aspect would echo that same feeling found in the Four of Cups. I suggest that the Four of Cups may show an opportunity being brought to her by the Queen of Pentacles, but the Four of Swords warns against overdoing it. Jacquelyn admits that she has burned herself out in the past overworking, although she herself is not the Queen of Pentacles. (Jacquelyn is a Queen of Cups–type personality and also a water sign.)

Another possibility is that she may not be overly enthused by what the Queen of Pentacles offers which means that both these fours represent an element of withdrawing from something. Strength, as the only major card, appears somewhat detached in the final position but brings an assurance of inner strength and the possibility of a better end position, perhaps without the situation the Queen of Pentacles brings. As the card of patience and quiet determination, following the Four of Swords, I feel the message here is also one of reminding her to pace herself and not become sidetracked. Perhaps the opportunity brought won't arrive at an appropriate time, or it may be something she cannot or does not wish to pursue, as it may not be all she first believes. Strength following here adds the patience and quiet determination needed to pursue the things that are important to her, so it would appear there is no rush, in the greater scheme of things.

One more four is found, as the Key card, representing someone prepared to work hard in order to achieve their aims, but with the reminder that sometimes a calculated risk needs to be taken in order to get things moving. The three fours in the reading within close proximity indicate structure and stability, although the energy they each work through is different. I feel the Four of Pentacles as the Key card shows Jacquelyn's ability to work hard but she needs to ensure that she does not burn herself out again as her business progresses. This advice circles back to the start of the personal area—the Ten of Wands and Nine of Swords—showing her tendency to worry and become overburdened. Jacquelyn states that as a yoga teacher, she is very conscious of the all-important balance, something she teaches in her stress and well-being workshops. Being self-employed she has recognised her tendency to take on work as it is offered, due to worrying about her diary's forward position and in the process, sometimes taking on too much.

Given the potential that exists in her reading I explain I can see how easy it would be for her to be heading towards the situation in her future position if she continually takes on other work. However, I hope that the reading has provided enough insight and confidence for her to be able to pace herself, rather than go like mad and burn out; her self-awareness of her own cycle is helpful. Jacquelyn agrees that sometimes we need reminding outside of ourselves of that which we already know. I nod knowingly—how true that is!

The Anchor
FUTURE AREA: TEMPERANCE

As if on cue Temperance provides an excellent end to the reading as the card of healing and balanced emotions. It further strengthens the message of patience and reminds Jacquelyn to apply moderation. This beautiful card brings harmony; the angel patiently blends fire and water, producing the alchemist's mix, a potent brew of perfectly balanced, combined energies. Jacquelyn feels this is a wonderful card to receive given her career, and says it embodies much of what she is trying to learn, teach, and attain. In sharing, she endeavours to enrich the lives of others.

Having completed the reading and summarised the details, I ask if there is anything further Jacquelyn would like to know. She says that from the reading, it would appear that her yoga is going to feature more than she anticipated and so would like to know more about this. We formulate the question as: "What is the future of my yoga business?"

Additional Spread: Celtic Cross

It's difficult to miss the Star at the end of this reading. Glancing at the other cards, things generally look safe enough but I will work through the reading from the beginning as always—just to be sure.

The Eight of Pentacles in the present position seems accurate as the "apprenticeship" card since Jacquelyn is developing and building her business. The Knight of Wands as the crossing card represents a change of residence, which ties in nicely, since she has changed the venue to her home area as the focal point. However, this card can also connect to a long journey (also note the Six of Swords as other people are viewing her—possible backup to this interpretation, suggesting distant travel).

The Ten of Wands in the third position with its message of heavy burdens shows how Jacquelyn has sometimes felt overburdened in the development of her business. From our previous interactions during her main reading we agree this card's meaning ties in well. The Page of Cups, who represents good news felt on an emotional level, further expands upon this interpretation. As Jacquelyn stated, when she receives news of further work she becomes excited and hits her highs, followed by the lows of an excessive workload—this is where she seeks to address her own balance. Quite appropriate cards to the history of her situation, aren't they?

In the most recent past, the Two of Cups shows a close and harmonious relationship; I ask if there is a reason why this would be here. Jacquelyn informs me that this was a relationship that she has recently let go but still remains a friendship.

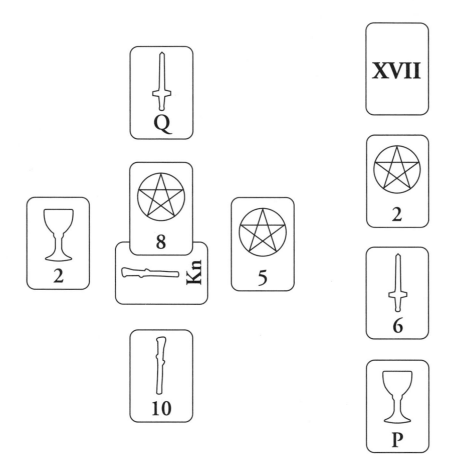

The Queen of Swords sits in her crowning thoughts. Having covered the description of this character earlier I do not feel it may be the same person to whom Jacquelyn connected in the Life Spread. The previous Queen of Swords appears to have exerted her energy already in connection with the Tower situation that has already happened.

The Two of Pentacles in the ninth position may provide deeper insight, as it shows successfully juggling more than one thing. Could this be her yoga business and the workshops? It's possible this lady is somehow connected to Jacquelyn's forward thoughts as they are related to these things. She confirms there is someone else she can associate with this card, someone she has thought about asking to help her run the workshops. The possibility is strong, although Jacquelyn seems to know quite a few ladies who fit the description of "inner strength, unafraid to speak out, champion of the underdog and—" Suddenly, realisation clicks. It turns out she is also sitting across from another person who fits the description. Jacquelyn has just been engaged to start teaching a yoga class at my health club (the very day before) which was how I came to ask if she would like to participate in this book! We both start laughing.

Moving on, the Five of Pentacles in the sixth position can represent financial loss, although it is surrounded by positive cards, which would make me opt more towards the meaning of possible financial hardship but also with the message to be careful not to miss an opportunity. As the Five leads to the Star, I suggest it is informing her that she may not see much initial financial reward. Sliding the Five up to sit beside the Star visually helps, as they sit alongside each other so well with their combined message. The Star is *the* reminder to have hope in the future and not to lose sight of her dreams; it is also a card of healing (excellent for the work she does) and can bring public recognition. Significantly, the Star has now appeared on three occasions, as it occupies the immediate future position in the Anchor and was also repeated in the previous reading of the Life Spread.

The Six of Swords in the eighth position, showing how other people view the situation, symbolises moving out of stormy waters into calmer times. It can also represent a journey, perhaps one that is long or over water, a meaning that could strengthen this same definition of the Knight of Wands.

The Page of Cups, bringing good news that will be felt on an emotional level, is a positive card in her apprehensions area.

Jacquelyn is quite amazed, as her initial thoughts had been that the workshops would lead to yoga, whereas she noted it appeared to play a more important role than she had first considered; she now wonders if it is from here that the other work will be generated. With this in mind she asks a further question: "Will the yoga lead to more work for her well-being workshops and booklet?"

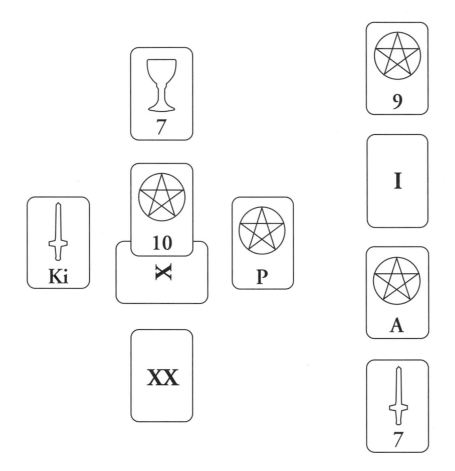

Additional Spread: Celtic Cross 2

The Ten of Pentacles in the first position often represents the family home and stability and is currently Jacquelyn's base for her yoga work. As the crossing card, the Wheel of Fortune brings a positive change of fortune with a new cycle commencing where progress can be made.

Judgement as the situation's past history indicates revival and points to connections with the past. Jacquelyn tells me that she has been developing the book and workshops over a period of years and some of her original clients were from the local area. She has also been practising yoga for more than twenty years and began her training with her teacher in her hometown too. This would all connect to the Judgement card. Interestingly enough, the Seven of Swords, balanced across in the seventh position, can represent an unexpected twist or the careful handling of some matter. In this instance the unexpected twist interpretation fits well.

I describe the King of Swords as a man connected to uniforms, the law, or government and ask if she has recently been dealing with anyone or anything of this nature in connection with her work. Jacquelyn states that her workbook has just received full accreditation and that a grant is now available for businesses to undertake her course with government funding. I remind her that Justice in the work area of the Anchor can represent contracts and agreements of a legal nature, something she could not initially place. The penny drops, as Jacquelyn now realises she is currently processing some contracts at the moment. With the King of Swords at the end of her work area from the original Life Spread, the indication is that there may be more work coming from this avenue in the future.

In her crowning thoughts, the Seven of Cups shows a situation where she feels many options are possible but she can be confused as to which one to pursue. Jacquelyn says this has been accurate in relation to her thoughts about which way to proceed with the yoga or the well-being workshops, though she feels her reading has revealed some helpful information in this regard. I explain that the Magician, which is also the central card of the Anchor, is balanced across from the Seven of Cups but has a stronger influence. The Magician shows that in the future she should lean more towards its interpretation of moving forward with confidence in her ability and that she should apply concentrated effort and willpower in order to succeed, suggesting a better sense of direction and focus.

In relation to Jacquelyn's question the Page of Pentacles seems most appropriate. Here, it brings goods news that should bring welcome changes, often with a financial or academic connection. With a direct connection to the final card (the Nine of Pentacles, symbolising financial increase), it represents material security and financial success. Very good news!

As other people are viewing the situation (the eighth position), the Ace of Pentacles could symbolise Jacquelyn's book or the founding of a business with potential to succeed materially. This is excellent news, given her question. An Ace found in positions five through nine also acts as a timing card. The Ace of Pentacles represents the period from the beginning of December and the Nine of Pentacles in the tenth position informs us that the ninth week from the beginning of December will be important to Jacquelyn's project in some way. Since the Ace is in the eighth position, it also tells us that this will somehow be reliant upon the actions of others and external forces.

The three cards in the "attitude" positions are mixed. The Seven of Cups is not a very decisive card to be driving her ambitions, since it tells of the indecisiveness associated with being caught up in imagining possibilities. However, this card is balanced against the Magician in the ninth position of hopes and wishes. As a major, it indicates that she will more likely be pulled in this direction, a much more positive influence. From our earlier discussion Jacquelyn is now aware of this and has taken it on board. A second seven in her apprehension area provides us with two sevens which can indicate changeability and a cycle change. As the card of speech, talk, and diplomacy it may also be a reminder to be careful in handling matters to ensure they go in the direction she wishes.

As you can see, I did not use the Reader's Fan in these Celtic Cross spreads, something that is entirely up to the reader. I hope that in doing so, it perhaps helps to demonstrate that it is not always necessary to attain suitable results from the Celtic Cross. Although the Reader's Fan can in some instances provide more background information of a situation, in Jacquelyn's case her main spread focused almost entirely on her work. As a result of our discussions, we had already gleaned sufficient background information. The cards in the Reader's Fan from the first Celtic Cross related to a personal background situation, which was not relevant to the main cards in her reading and she preferred not to disclose them here.

Overall this was a very positive reading that answered Jacquelyn's question, clarified her priorities, and gave her the focus needed to achieve the best result for her business. The Star made an appearance in a future position in three of her four spreads, indicating some wonderful possibilities ahead.

Jacquelyn is delighted with her reading. Whereas she had previously considered her yoga as something completely enjoyable but in certain respects secondary, she now realises it is the root and basis that establishes and promotes herself and the well-being workshops. Whilst the two are inextricably linked (the workshops contain many yoga aspects), the way to achieve her aims is the opposite of how she had originally thought. Realising this now, she will review the way she considers her business in the future.

Results and Feedback

Two Months Later

Jacquelyn is pleased with how business is going and has just had some exciting new offers materialise in rapid succession. She tells me that a couple of days ago, she was approached to go to the States to do some work with their military. When I ask her where the offer came from, she informed me it had originated through a military officer who had attended one of her yoga classes just this week. As this linked to the King of Swords (a man in uniform, or connection to the government) who featured at the end of her work area in the Life Spread, I said there should have been something important from another man before this, the King of Pentacles. "Yes," she said, "I was just going to tell you about that."

It just so happened that the week before we were to have our follow-up, she had received another offer from a successful landowner with international business interests. He has a large work force based in another country and wanted her to go there to work with them. Jacquelyn recounted that both offers had originated from yoga work based in her home area, involved international connections and working abroad, and would feature her workshop and book incorporating yoga. Things were starting to shape up nicely and she felt as if everything had finally taken off (Knight of Pentacles and Knight of Swords).

Looking back over Jacquelyn's readings, a number of the indications were repeated and tie in well with the results she is experiencing.

Three Months Later

Jacquelyn has recently met someone and things are going very well. How did this happen? She met him through attending a group activity of her daughter's; he was the parent of another child present. It seems that the family aspect from the Ten of Pentacles leading to the Star played a more significant role than first imagined (relationship area of the Life Spread).

Four Months Later

So far, everything has seemed to evolve nicely, leaving only the Queen of Pentacles situation unaccounted for in the reading. When I asked Jacquelyn about it she informed me there had been the possibility to tie in with another lady's business in a different way. Due to varying events these plans had been delayed and eventually faded, although she stated that she wasn't troubled by it because it had no effect on her main business.

In Jacquelyn's Own Words
I felt I was at a crossroads, and the reading helped me identify areas where I could follow up; the outcome confirmed things to me that were very helpful. I also met someone romantically who I felt featured in the reading. Overall the results were very optimistic and encouraged me to focus on yoga as the base of my business.

Reader's Tips
Recording Readings

Some readers like to record the session so the seeker can take it with them to listen and process later. I have found that a lot of private information comes out in a session, and it is not usually the type people want to share, or want others to inadvertently hear.

Even though I informed everyone at the beginning that the recorder was purely for my use in typing up their case study and would be deleted immediately after use, at some point in the reading a large proportion of them asked, "This is private, isn't it? No one else will hear this, will they?" Before discussing anything personal, they would immediately glance at the recorder first and ask the question. There was, in every instance, personal information shared or revealed that the seeker did not want disclosed. I found this enlightening, considering everyone knew their reading would be published and was the reason for them being there.

You never know what is going to come out in a reading session; the depth of information can be surprising. You can provide a better guarantee of privacy and an environment where the seeker feels more comfortable and relaxed to talk with you candidly by not recording the reading but as with everything, the choice is yours. I know some people like to take a recording of the reading but it was so noticeable from the case studies that I felt it worth mentioning for you to consider.

11
The Rock Band

Heaven's Basement is a five-piece male British rock band that has toured alongside Papa Roach, Shinedown, and Buckcherry just to name a few you may be familiar with. The band works full-time—this is their professional occupation. At the moment they are unsigned but have interest from numerous record companies.

I had never done a reading for a group and was wondering how I could apply it where the band itself was an entity in its own right. I needed the energy of one of the band members to shuffle the cards and ask the questions, as I felt this would provide the best result. I also wanted to be sure that the reading we received would not be related to only the individual concerned. Since the band member would be the one handling the cards, how could I be certain the reading would not completely refer to situations in his own life?

My plan of campaign had been to use the longest standing member of the group and select a significator card to represent the band itself. This presented a further question of which card to use. Since this was a different type of situation for me I was unsure which card would be appropriate and I also wanted to be careful not to remove a card from the deck that could be of importance if it appeared in the reading. None of my interpretations really pointed to group activities in this manner, so I turned to my bookshelf to glean insight from what other authors had to say. In Rachel Pollack's *Tarot Wisdom: Spiritual Teachings and Deeper Meanings* I found the answer. It seemed perfect. Rachel states that for her the general theme of the three is group activities. "Thus the Three of Wands could be people sharing creative activities." In readings the interpretation supplied stated, "Energy manifested, coming to an understanding of what creative energy has meant in your life. Exciting group action." This sounded precisely like what I was looking for!

The next problem I encountered was trying to get together with the band. After three months of various tours, our paths only crossed twice, and on both occasions it was fairly much a case of them falling into bed following a gig and back out the door the next morning. The third occasion was a gig itself, so they were performing, and then spent some time speaking to fans before disappearing in the van to travel to the next venue.

I was starting to get anxious about the reading and whether there would be enough time to collect the results for the book, but when the reading went ahead it was in a completely unexpected and unintentional way. I know the group because my son is the bassist, but at the time he was also the newest member of the band, not the person we had decided upon using. Additionally, despite growing up around Tarot cards, Rob has never had nor wanted a reading—he has always said he would prefer not to know. When he joined Heaven's Basement, I realised it would be an interesting reading to include, and when approached the other band members, they were all in favour. Realising I was starting to get really concerned about time issues (or more accurately, I was getting quite stressed) Rob surprised me when he volunteered to do the reading for the band before leaving for tour that night. Wow, two birds with one stone!

In order to avoid the confusion of personal issues turning up in the group reading, I had decided that I would first do a Life Spread and Anchor for the individual who would be doing the asking on behalf of the band. This way, I felt that any personal issues or situations would show up for them and I would know if the Celtic Cross was addressing the question asked, or whether it was still focussing upon an important situation for the individual.

The intention had not been to publish the spreads for the individual and only to focus on the group question. However, there was one area of the Life Spread that did not fit into Rob's reading, appearing in the personal area, which we felt must be connected to the group, due to the cards present.

The Life Spread
PERSONAL AREA

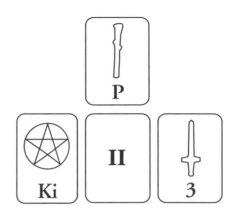

The Page of Wands suggests that the news concerns work. The King of Pentacles we cannot place (in addition to the five band members there are also a manager, agent, and various road, sound, and stage crew to consider). The High Priestess indicates there is information as yet unknown that will soon be unveiled, resulting in conflict or the possibility of separation, shown by the Three of Swords.

I explain to Rob that the High Priestess often refers to secrecy, although this in itself is not necessarily negative, as the secrets she reveals are usually of benefit once known. Similarly, though the news coming in could cause conflict or separation in some way, it does not always lead to a full split.

Since this information was in Rob's personal area, I felt the situation would not take long to show itself, and the cards appeared to read as a straight grouping of one event. It seemed that one member of the band could be announcing he wanted to leave, or something he revealed could lead to conflict. Alternatively, it could be related to their manager or agent, since we have no idea who the King of Pentacles is.

The Anchor

Whilst the Anchor was part of Rob's personal spread there are a few points worth mentioning that appear to relate specifically to the band. He was happy to share them with us here.

The Fool in the first position was most accurate as to how he came to be a part of Heaven's Basement. The opportunity of the audition came from out the blue and was completely unexpected. By the time he had arrived home from the audition the band informed him he was successful, but he had only a couple of days to prepare everything to leave on tour for Germany—initially we understood he would have three weeks. It had required a major choice on his part, as he had a secure job at the time. The Fool certainly took him down a completely new pathway.

The Empress in the work area was also very accurate—success through nurturing something to fruition. Rob had studied music at college for a number of years, taught with his original tutors, and had been in another band previously, meeting Heaven's Basement on the circuit.

In the heart of the matter, the Hierophant, which can represent large organisations, was also the central card in his work area of the Life Spread. Justice, in the immediate future, could represent contracts.

The Celtic Cross

The Three of Wands was taken out of the deck to use as the significator to represent the band and placed in the centre of the table. They currently have a number of labels interested in signing them, but it was decided to take a broader approach with the question to see what might lie ahead for the band due to the cards indicating separation. I asked him to shuffle the remaining deck whilst concentrating on the band and the question, "What is the future of Heaven's Basement?"

The first thing I noticed is that six out of the ten cards are from the major arcana—very powerful! The card in the first position shows what the band is experiencing in relation to the question. The Empress indicates fruitfulness and success through nurturing; being crossed by the World (and having already overviewed all the other cards) is also an excellent "filter" to act as the crossing card, so we have a repeated message, although slightly more powerful, of assured success. The World also tends to indicate success that results from a long period of work, so we can see how these two cards complement one another. I also find it very interesting that the Empress makes an appearance, as it often represents motherhood or parenting; the band members all have excellent support from their families.

The basis of the situation, the Wheel of Fortune, has provided some good opportunities that accompanied the band's hard work, bringing them to their current position. The Wheel shows the commencement of a new chapter beginning and is very positively aspected by the surrounding cards.

In the most recent past, the Three of Cups shows growth and abundance but also indicates they should have been celebrating some happy news. Rob cannot place this. There have been a number of good things happening but nothing that they have actually celebrated. Just recently they were informed that the main support group for a forthcoming tour with Theory of a Deadman in Europe had withdrawn and their agent had put Heaven's Basement forward as the replacement, but they have not yet received confirmation. Whilst the band is excited about the prospect they know it remains only a possibility until confirmed. I inform Rob that

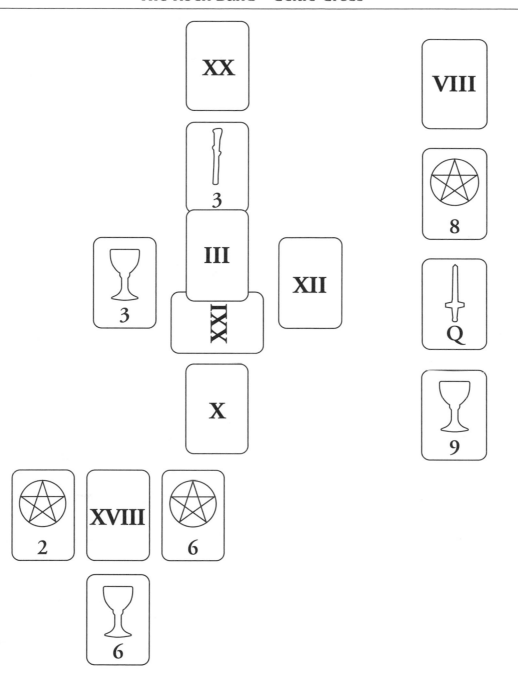

they should hear within the next week or two, since the energy of this card is already in the process of moving.

The crowning card perhaps becomes more meaningful, combining the three "attitude" cards: Judgement, the Nine of Cups, and the Eight of Pentacles. Read on their most basic level, we can see the desire for fulfilment of their wishes from the Nine, perfecting the skills of their trade in the Eight, and working with the results of previous seeds planted—as Judgement is often known as the "karmic" card, driving their thoughts and actions.

Those of us outside the music industry tend to think that the entire goal of a band is to become signed to a record company but it isn't that straightforward. Contracts are legally binding, so it is important that the future considerations of both parties are felt to be mutually beneficial to everyone's goals. Various record labels cater to different genres and work differently with their artists, so it is important to be signed to the right one where hopefully a long, fruitful, and mutually beneficial business relationship will follow.

I explain to Rob that I feel the Hanging Man in the sixth position of the immediate future could be connected to the situation that had shown in his personal area, since it hadn't yet happened and could certainly cause a rethink. Whilst it can suggest a feeling of things being in suspension, the Hanging Man is quite the card of the unconventional which I felt was appropriate, given the band's image. Since the final card is still promising, and the reading is working through the filter of the World, I explained that I felt the Hanging Man might be informing them that they need to look at things from a different perspective in order to find the right solution to move forward in the future. Further sacrifices may be necessary in order to get to where they want to be and it could be that for a while they might feel as if they are treading water but I strongly felt the main message was related to how they review everything.

The Queen of Swords is also an interesting card in the eighth position; could this be the partner of the unknown person about to make their announcement? Whoever she may be, this lady feels quite strongly about the situation, although we cannot tell if this is in a positive or negative light since we only have the court card itself. It would not be unreasonable to think that if one of the band members were about to leave, his partner would have an opinion concerning their decision.

It all sounds very glamorous, doesn't it—being in a rock band, touring the world with well-known names, and playing for excited audiences. Perhaps we have a distorted view with recent contestant-centric television programmes that show what appears to be instant fame.

For young people of course it is an exciting lifestyle, granting the opportunity to do what they love, hanging out with people they enjoy being with…when things are going well.

As with everything there is a downside. The early days for bands working their way up the circuit is quite tough going. They have little or no money, live out of suitcases, sleep on floors, the van, or possibly a bed, and time is mainly spent travelling, away from family or partners for extended periods. It takes time to build a fan base so venues know the band is worth booking (ticket sales) and band members do all of this themselves until they get to a point where they have proven their worth so an agent and manager will work with them. This is all in addition to rehearsals, writing new material, recording, etc. It can be a long haul and there are often casualties along the way, so it really is a labour of love. In this instance, the original band formed in 2008. Talk about chasing the dream! Having gotten to this point we can see the importance of those first three cards.

Strength in the final position is encouraging. In *Understanding Aleister Crowley's Thoth Tarot,* Lon Milo DuQuette gives part of the interpretation for this card as "Courage, strength, energy and action." Similarly, Dr. Arthur Edward Waite, from the *Rider Waite Tarot Deck* interprets the card as, "Power, energy, action, courage; magnanimity." As such, I think we can conclude that this is a good card to complete the reading!

The Hanging Man may suggest that the success they are hoping for may not come as quickly as they would like, and Strength hints that they are going to have to keep working with courage, quiet determination, and endurance. If they can keep their eye on their vision, that strength has the power to pull them through. The World as the atmosphere card works in their favour. The final two future cards, in comparison to the original starting position of the Empress and Wheel of Fortune, also indicate that in the future it may feel a bit tougher than where they are now.

I feel that the answer, reason, and understanding of why we have the Hanging Man probably lies in the cards from Rob's personal area of the Life Spread. At this stage, any band member leaving or change in agent/management would be a setback. However, Strength is still an excellent card. I am reminded that it is also a card of sexual attraction and magnetism, so whilst the fan base is a mix of both genders, for an all-male rock band in the world of entertainment, it's quite a helpful ingredient!

The Reader's Fan, with the Moon placed between the Two and Six of Pentacles, seemed to show the close but shifting balancing act everyone must make to keep the band going and moving forwards. The Six of Cups re-emphasises the importance of the Judgement card, with the overlapping interpretation of past aspects that had brought them together.

Results and Feedback

The Next Day

Upon returning for rehearsals, the lead singer announced he needed to take some time out for personal reasons and was uncertain whether he would be staying. The other band members were stunned by his news—and the card's accuracy. (I was suitably gobsmacked!)

The band had been together a number of years, and all its members are good friends. Everyone was understandably upset by the news. The week was spent in consultation with management and, as the future of his position was undecided, it was agreed that for the moment there would be no announcement whilst a potential replacement was quietly sought. Should the lead singer leave for good, it was understood that promotion companies could still cancel their future tours. All the cards from the personal area of Rob's reading fit together here and we can also see both aspects of the interpretation given for the High Priestess, the secret being revealed but also the one being kept.

When they telephoned me with the news I reiterated the future cards of the band's reading. I recalled the Hanging Man in the immediate future and suggested it would be a good idea to keep a completely open mind regarding people they auditioned, as a new lead singer could come from an alternative genre, be someone they might not normally consider, or could come to them in an unconventional way.

Ten Days Later

The band received confirmation that they would be playing main support to Theory of a Deadman on their European tour. So the Three of Cups and the timing of this news proved accurate.

One Month Later

Heaven's Basement has found a vocalist from another band who will work with them and stand in for the next tour. The band has just announced the news, which has also allowed them to now advertise publicly for a vocalist. Whilst the first tour will go ahead as planned, the future is unsettled until a permanent replacement is found. The Hanging Man begins in their immediate future; a period of feeling that life is in suspension.

Four Months Later

With the first couple of tours completed, Heaven's Basement spent a solid week in auditions. Whilst a few potentials have been spotted, the band members are not sure they have ultimately found who they are looking for. Meanwhile further bookings are still coming in from their agent with some exciting venues and names on the close horizon, creating further urgency to find their vocalist.

Whilst taking a few days off, they searched online to see if they could find the right person. They found a singer they feel may fit the bill but upon contacting him, they learn he is heavily pursuing a solo career. After auditions and meetings they decide to do a trial period, to see how things work out. The new singer is to join them on the next leg of a tour. Everyone is hopeful the new arrangement may work. Rehearsals begin and the tour continues.

Six Months Later

You start to wonder when something is going to go right! Shortly before the end of the tour one of the guitarists broke his fingers prior to a performance, so the band continued as a four-piece. On top of this, it was mutually decided that professionally the new singer just wasn't the right person for Heaven's Basement and he returned to continue his solo career.

I was quite concerned at what the next phone call would bring and wondered whether they would be losing heart by now. Given the circumstances, I was surprised by their upbeat attitude and determination. Having discussed the matter at length they remain committed to the band and its future. If anything, the members feel the challenges have strengthened their resolve. As a result of recent events they feel two things have become evident; the first is that the four-piece worked better than they had anticipated, and the second was how much support they have around them.

Following a meeting with their manager and agent it has been suggested they audition vocalists from within the music industry (for which supportive contacts are already making phone calls) and write some new material that will be better suited to the new vocalist. Along with some interesting recommendations that cannot be revealed here yet, it sounds like some Hanging Man thinking at its best! However, what is most noticeable is how much this card has prolonged the proceedings.

The grit and resolve from Strength is certainly showing although there is still a ways to go yet. Having ended the previous year so close to achieving their goals the start to this year was quite a setback. The band is no stranger to adversity, however, and seems to power its way through, regardless of whatever lands.

Eight Months Later

In the latest phone call the band tells me they are taking a well-earned break from constant touring to take stock and do some creative work in the studio. At the moment they are actively auditioning vocalists, with the intention of spending the next few months writing and rehearsing with the new singer, and hope to emerge guns blazing in 2011.

Stop the Presses!

Just as the manuscript was going off to the publisher I received news that the band believed they had found the right vocalist. Although it is still early, so far everything appears to be coming together well. It has been nine months since the original reading, so it has taken this long to work past the delay of the Hanging Man. Another interesting point worth noting lies in the connection between Judgement (position 5) and the Eight of Pentacles (position 9). This vocalist had applied when the band very first advertised but cancelled his audition due to other commitments at the time; he contacted them again and subsequently auditioned later, as his circumstances had changed.

As this book goes to print (seventeen months after the original reading), I am pleased to report that the first tour with their new line-up and material was a great success. Everyone is relieved and delighted! Heaven's Basement is now in advanced negotiations with a record label. You can stay tuned to their continuing story on Facebook and at www.heavensbasement.com with music, news, tour dates, and photographs.

In Heaven's Basement's Own Words

When the reading was initially done for us we didn't think too much about the results, but as the weeks and months went on we found it to be more and more accurate! This helped, as we knew we were in a period of transition and growth and that we would ultimately come out stronger.

The reading was definitely a good thing for us as it maintained our belief in what we are doing through tough periods … and removing the negative cards from our website was definitely a smart move! (Author's note: see the Reader's Tip.)

Reader's Tips
An Interesting Tale of Symbolism

When I first saw the Heaven's Basement's official website, I was quite concerned. Whoever designed it had embedded some of the most negative Tarot cards as graphic images. It may all seem harmless pop culture, and quite fitting for a rock band, but the meanings of the chosen cards that were grouped together made me feel uncomfortable.

A large image of the Tower was used as the background of the main site, which stayed in the frame as you navigated around. In between various titles there were images of four cards grouped together: the Tower, Death, the Devil, and the Eight of Swords. I contacted the group and explained that these cards together can bring the worst kind of bad news imaginable and, whether they believed in symbolism or not, I thought it would be advisable to remove them in case they attracted the negative energy they represented. Initially, I think they took my comments with good humour but not very seriously, although they did ask the web designer to remove them. They were told it was quite a big job to take them down and so the images remained for quite some time.

In the time I have known Heaven's Basement, the original bass player left and the stand-in broke his wrist just before they were due to leave for a European tour. They have had numerous travel problems and accidents including a breakdown in Germany where they were stuck for five days which resulted in missed gigs, a tyre blow-out in Holland, and another at top speed in the outside lane on the way to a gig in the UK—that one shook them up as it was serious and they realised it could have been fatal. The lead singer left at the most promising time and they lost their long-standing rehearsal rooms. Song tracks they had been waiting for from their producer were continually delayed and were needed to send to record companies. Personally, I felt that was a big enough list.

Given the bad luck and misfortune they were experiencing I mentioned my concerns to the group again, this time the Tower was removed from the background. They were surprised when almost immediately the soundtracks they had been waiting for arrived after eight months.

Is it all just coincidence? Well, that is for you to decide. Personally I wouldn't choose to display cards to represent myself that I wouldn't like to see in my own reading. An interesting tale worth consideration, don't you think?

12

The One That Got Away!

This one could equally have been entitled "Following Your Own Advice," or perhaps more appropriately, "Eating Your Own Words." The intention was to provide a reading for someone I knew well, as most readers are asked to read for close friends.

Maureen is a dance teacher, a former professional dancer with the grace of a gazelle and the wonderful Glaswegian wit and humour of Billy Connolly. Being a good sport, she volunteered to bare her soul for you and have her reading done; her life journey has been an interesting one.

It was the week before Christmas and the weather was dreadful. I wondered whether Maureen would make it through, as the heavy snow and icy conditions made my small village difficult to access, but she duly arrived, triumphantly producing mince pies for the occasion. I put the kettle on, and warmed and plated the unexpected treat, whilst she set to work shuffling the cards. All the while, Maureen chatted away about Christmas shopping and other incidental nuances of life.

When I laid the cards out we both looked surprised (me more so) at the complete mess filled with Swords and other wonderful pleasantries. They appeared a total jumble. Given the strange problems I had encountered earlier with my deck (that I mentioned on page 3 in the Introduction) and the fact she hadn't been concentrating upon the task at hand, I gathered them up and gave the deck back to her for shuffling, this time whilst silently concentrating. I have the sneaking suspicion you may have guessed what followed from here—cringe moment!

I cannot even present to you the spread in the order that first appeared because I never recorded it. My recollection of it was an unpleasant mixture of troubling and disruptive influences across the board. What I can tell you is that the second set of cards that I duly did record and read bore no resemblance to the events that followed, aside from the Tower in the immediate future of the Anchor. Suffice to say, the kind of picture the original cards painted were clearly more in line with what happened next in Maureen's life, which rather left me eating a different kind of pie … namely of the humble variety! As you can imagine, I felt terrible but thankfully Maureen was fine with everything; this may not have been the case had she been a paying client and not a close friend.

Reader's Tips
(And a Note to Self)

I recall mentioning in *Easy Tarot* to read the first cards that are lain down, resisting the temptation to do them again, since the first cards drawn are usually the most accurate. Everything considered, it would appear that was fairly good advice. If only I had followed it!

However, it was an interesting insight for me as the original cards had still produced the relevant information, despite the fact that most conditions we recommend following fell by the wayside on this occasion. It is said that experience is the best teacher, but most particularly if it is someone else's. I hope that by highlighting my error it helps you to avoid a similar situation in your own reading experiences.

13
Summary of the Readings

*I*t was not intended to investigate a full analysis, or post-mortem, on the readings once they were finished. Indeed, there is quite a difference in being able to study the cards at leisure, as opposed to reading situations where you find yourself in the hot seat. Our focus in this book was more from the practice aspect, rather than the theoretical stance I mentioned earlier. However, there were a few experiences that stood out from comparisons found within the readings that seemed worthy of further note. Before delving into them, I would like to quickly recap the seeker's involvement in the reading.

Seeker Involvement

The case studies provided the essence of how to engage and receive the involvement and interaction of the seeker, as these readings have been presented as a way of working together in order to help them. Creating the right balance in a two-way conversation relies upon how you handle the situation, ensuring the required flow of information at the right times; enough to verify what you need to know but not too much too soon that it may colour your thinking.

Here are some *loose* guidelines from a theoretical stance (for as we have seen from the case studies, each reading differs).

- Cover the format the reading will take before you begin. This way the seeker knows what to expect and their active role within the reading.

- You can start "cold" from the basis card of the Anchor, outlining the interpretations and then asking the seeker to verify if they can associate with this quite recently.

- Whichever area you move to in the Life Spread, use the same approach with the key/consolidation card in the area.

- Next, see if that card links to the first card of the trio underneath the Key card. Usually these cards provide the background situation of the seeker's most recent past and present.

- Let the seeker know that based on the cards you have in front of you, you are trying to establish where you are in the timeline of events in their life. Try not to move further forward, reading the future of the situation, until you feel that the cards in that area reflect what the seeker believes is his or her circumstances.

- If they cannot place events, the cards presented may all be referring to a future situation that is developing. However, as we have seen, sometimes the seeker does not make an association at the time, only later to verify something you referred to earlier.

- If the seeker cannot connect with that area at first, you can move on to another area, taking the same approach until you find your flow and make the connection.

- Ask people to expand on details or enlighten you when you need them to—don't be afraid to ask.

- If the seeker is not talking to you, or he or she responds in monosyllables, they may have misinterpreted what you need from them; they may also be quite nervous. Gently re-emphasise that you require their feedback or use the point above—ask them to expand upon their response, or ask further questions.

- Share relevant cards with them from their reading by handing a card to them whilst you explain the meaning or ask them to describe what they see. This can act as a good icebreaker and can also serve to help them retain the message of a particular card after they have left.

Each seeker is different but there will come a point in the reading where you can tell they feel more comfortable with you and the reading situation—the conversation starts to flow.

Role of the Key Card:
Seeing a Different Picture

You have heard me refer to the Life Spread as similar to opening a door or looking through windows into the seeker's life. In dream interpretations and Jungian psychology theory, a house represents the structure of someone's life and its rooms reflect different aspects of it. If you look at the layout of the Life Spread you will note that it resembles the early pictures that children draw of a house, with a door in the middle and two windows on either side, top and bottom. The picture invariably contains a tree to the side of the house (the Anchor) and a pathway leading to the front door (the personal area of the Life Spread). In many ways, the Key card is that pathway.

Whilst the Key card has always been involved in the reading I have never had the opportunity to analyse its importance in a way that distinguished its part more distinctly. Previously I had regarded it as a somewhat free-flowing aspect that may be applied in varying ways but its purpose was not very clear. However, due to the comparisons found from doing this study, I will be trying a different approach in the future, as it revealed an insightful position within the reading and the seeker's life.

The Key card in each of the Life Spread readings shows us the atmosphere of the pathway the seeker was travelling at the time of the reading. Whilst our starting point of the basis card from the Anchor shows events that have recently happened or are occurring around the seeker, the Key card of the Life Spread shows us what they are presently *experiencing* in their life.

Once the readings were concluded, I compared the Key card from the Life Spread to what the seeker was experiencing at the time of the reading. From the information that became known to us the relevance of this card becomes a little clearer:

- Chapter 2: Five of Cups—fears over past regrets with the relationship.
- Chapter 3: Judgement—results of past actions; concerns over court case.
- Chapter 4: Two of Pentacles—balancing different aspects of her life.
- Chapter 5: Ten of Swords—the recent ending of her relationship.
- Chapter 7: Four of Cups—her nonchalant attitude and reason for it.
- Chapter 8: Knight of Wands—living between two homes and desire to move.
- Chapter 9: The Lovers—the relationship and business connection.
- Chapter 10: Four of Pentacles—working hard towards goals.

Since this did not become fully evident to me until afterwards I purposely did not alter my original references regarding this card in other sections of the book. With this consideration we can view position twenty-one as the literal "key to the door" that unlocks the personal area and our entry into the structure of their life, the experience of their psyche and the pathway of their current emotions.

Similar Patterns and Influences

Chasing the Dream

There was a remarkable resemblance found in the results in the Celtic Cross spreads for Heaven's Basement and Reid Rosenthal. Not only did Strength conclude both readings but the Hanging Man featured in the sixth position for Heaven's Basement and the eighth position for Reid, who also had the Two of Swords in the sixth.

Both readings are for people following an ambition, chasing a goal that will rely upon recognition and support in the public arena, namely: music, and writing and publishing. These fields are difficult to break into; competition is fierce and success can be limited. Given the similarity of their aspirations, and the meaning of the cards featured, it is not unreasonable to consider that to succeed will require persistence, determination, endurance, and the revised plans en route signalled by the Hanging Man. Interestingly enough, such qualities are usually found in successful people.

In other scenarios, Strength can also make an appearance when people are in challenging situations, whether emotional or professional. The card may signal a long haul, where the result is reliant upon the seeker demonstrating the required characteristics in order to accomplish an objective. The Hanging Man can slow things down with its suspension interpretation, so the combination of both cards can produce a delaying effect, although the messages they carry provide excellent guidance in the pursuit of success. However, in instances where Strength appeared as the final card, the importance of the creative and unconventional, "think outside the box" aspect of the Hanging Man became an important component towards the destination. As my readings do not usually cover a timeframe outside twelve months, it would be interesting to see what their position reveals at that time and what a new reading would reveal then.

Strength is a powerful card that can signify success as a result of persistence. This card's energy is a bit easier than the Chariot, which can indicate triumph over obstacles—suggesting there will be some and possibly a bumpy ride! Strength is the card of unwavering determination, but wouldn't you have just loved to see those readings culminating with the Sun?

Indicators of Success in the Life Spread

When you find the Sun and the World together in the Life Spread's combination of four cards, success of the significant variety is not far away, as long as they appear with other cards relating to the situation or additional positive cards. When accompanied by the Wheel of Fortune and the Star, success is fairly assured and should literally be around the corner.

When Laura (chapter 4) first came to me for a reading, she was just entering the world of modelling; the cards in her work area featured the Nine of Cups, the Sun, the Star, and the World. Her success in breaking into this industry happened quite quickly, resulting in national press and television appearances soon after.

While mulling over the idea and plucking up the courage to send the manuscript of my first book to Llewellyn for consideration, the cards in the Life Spread (again in the work section) were the Ace of Pentacles, the World, the Wheel of Fortune, and the Sun.

These cards also translate into personal circumstances and love situations, as I have seen these cards featured in the home area of the Life Spread, with the Ten of Cups, the Sun, the Lovers, and the World, and similar configurations in the love area.

As mentioned in the first section of this book, these are some of the scenarios when the cards from a group appear to speak as one. Instances like this do occur and appear so outstanding you tend not to forget them.

The only cautionary note I would add here is to keep the cards in context with the person's lifestyle or activities. The success indicators usually show an event that will be highly significant to the seeker in a way that would be defined as outside of their usual experience. Success is measured in different ways and varying degrees. For instance, a highly successful business transaction would translate differently for someone with an annual turnover of a hundred thousand, versus someone who normally deals in multi-million transactions. The relevance of the impact upon the person is not lessened, as in either case you know you are looking at something that will be considered "big news."

Of Past Regrets and Differing Viewpoints

The Five of Cups made a number of appearances and highlighted a few emotional disappointments but two of the case studies featured the Five of Cups and the Hanging Man quite strongly, in central positions, and both were connected to relationship situations.

Laura presented the Hanging Man as the first card of the Life Spread, with the Five of Cups central to her home area. Sarah (chapter 5) had the Hanging Man in the central position of the

Anchor, with the Five of Cups central to the love area. Both women had recently experienced breakups and reconciliation had featured. Although their circumstances and outcomes were different, both reflected upon and mentioned these cards in our subsequent conversations.

In relationship situations where the Five of Cups appears I have not found it unusual for the Hanging Man to feature somewhere, if not right alongside. Given the nature of an emotional split, both aspects of the Hanging Man are often pertinent; the feeling of dangling in mid-air that often accompanies a break-up is the first indication. However, if there is any possibility of the relationship being reconciled, it is realistic to suggest that healing rifts often involve the ability to move past a particular viewpoint in order to find common ground, so it would seem a necessary ingredient.

It perhaps should not be surprising how frequently the Hanging Man makes an appearance in reading situations, as most people who consult the cards come looking for an answer to a predicament they are experiencing. Often the answer to their problem will involve stepping back from the situation and viewing it differently in order to move forward.

Perhaps for those involved in creative endeavours, as just covered with the two case studies chasing success, indulging in some lateral thinking goes with the territory and becomes familiar in the process. The Hanging Man presents not only the sense of feeling suspended within a dilemma but also offers the answer to movement away from the problem, by encouraging an enlightened perspective.

Secrets and Skulduggery

The various cards that represent secrecy present it in different ways and, as always, the indications of their effect in the seeker's life relies upon the messages found in surrounding cards. As we have seen, secrets are not always negative, for it is the rare person who lives life with every facet presented as an open book—most prefer to maintain a degree of privacy to certain details. Generally, the High Priestess reveals secrets that will be to our benefit. The Moon informs us that more is happening beneath the surface that will emerge in due course, though when surrounded by less favourable cards may indicate deception. The Devil can represent secret plans that can swing either way, again depending upon surrounding cards—and then there is the Five of Swords.

As we have seen from the different results found in the case studies, whenever the Five of Swords appeared, it led to a situation where someone was up to no good and not in the seeker's interest. Of all the secrecy cards, this is the one to watch for when something untoward is happening. Due to the nature of the card's message, it is something the seeker is usually unaware of and, unfortunately, it frequently connects to people around them they thought could be trusted. However, when these cards appear grouped together and this Five is amongst them, there is usually trouble of a greater degree brewing on the horizon.

Laura had the Devil, High Priestess, and Five of Swords all grouped together in her work area. It was a situation she was completely unaware of and, in that instance, the Five of Swords was at the end of the trio. Fortunately, there were good indications found in the Anchor of her reading and the situation was not further reflected elsewhere. In the other readings, the Five had passed or was contained.

Though the Five of Swords is a minor card, it can lead to surprising and unpleasant damage—always one to watch for. From my experiences with this card it's one I rank right up alongside the Tower, as left unchecked I have seen it develop into the kind of situations none of us would willingly invite. However, if the effects of this card have not yet manifested, it is usually not too difficult to unearth the source of the problem. Should this card present itself in a future position of a reading, measures can be taken to prevent the effect; it immediately raises awareness, opens your eyes, gets you digging, and pushes you to take the necessary preventative action.

The surrounding cards will often provide further information on the affected area and sometimes even the people who may be involved. Having been in business for a long time I have been subject to attempted take-over bids, client and business poaching (or theft), and it has always been this card that has made me aware when something untoward was brewing. Once alerted it provides the opportunity to head off the problem. Whilst I may not like this card, it has helped to successfully prevent some damaging situations, both for others and myself. The Five of Swords is a warning to "watch your back" when someone around you is plotting dishonest dealings that are not to your benefit. It is not uncommon to find this card around successful executives, or those whose position generates envy from others, so it often features in matters involving business or corporate politics. Nevertheless, it can present itself in any manner of various situations, with the surrounding cards informing the seeker of where to focus their attention. Forewarned is often forearmed with this one.

Heroes and Villains

Ah, the court cards, our unsung heroes of the piece who never failed us! I appreciate that people use the courts in many different ways that can reflect our varying natures, but by applying them as specific personalities, it narrowed down their application when reading for divination purposes. In reality, most of us know or come into contact with more than four men and women of different personas, so the biggest risk is remembering that in future positions, the King or Queen may be someone the seeker has yet to meet. Yet otherwise, as players on the stage of life they performed their part so well, at least sufficiently that if you previously struggled with them, it may provide some confidence of their appearance in your future reading situations.

There is only one reading that has not featured amongst the others as planned, and that was a self-reading. As this book developed, it became apparent that space would not allow for mine to be an element within it. However, this seems an appropriate moment to share a relevant tale with you, as you shall see.

Josie's Celtic Cross

Whilst writing this book, a friend invited me to visit. This had become something of a long-standing joke between us, as despite numerous plans over the years our hectic schedules have ensured these meetings never materialised. It was therefore with some surprise that I found myself booking the ticket for the long journey this multi-flight trip entails. Perhaps less surprised when British Airways promptly announced their strike and the Icelandic volcanic ash cloud situation erupted, literally!

Things were not looking good, so I checked with the Tarot about my planned trip. Here are the cards from that part of my reading.

My daughter walked in as I was observing the response and, after asking what my question was, she commiserated with me over what appeared to be a non-starter. I could not place the King of Cups, although I know a few who match this description, including my son and an ex. Sitting resolutely at the end, whoever he was, he seemed responsible for the Death card and it didn't look good. However, time marched on, the situation did not manifest and the reading faded from my mind amidst the chaos of arrangements and packing. Going away is never a straightforward occurrence for me!

Meanwhile, my flights were rearranged, the ash cloud subsided, and I began the first leg of my long-delayed visit. With both Tarot and manuscript safely tucked away, all was well.

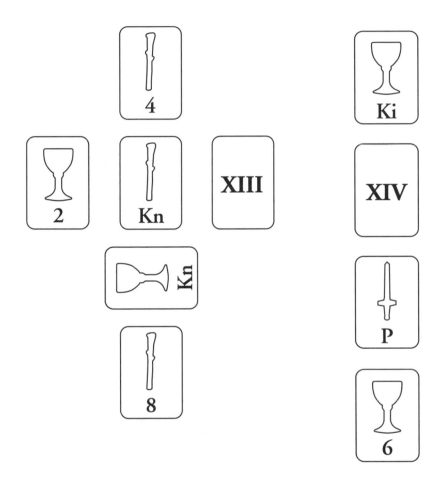

The intention had been to spend time catching up, relaxing, and some uninterrupted writing—total bliss!

Within a couple of days of my arrival there were some rumblings regarding an important business transaction my friend was involved with, so I offered to do his cards. The plethora of court cards that appeared in those readings fit the description of the people concerned, all unknown to me, and it seemed he was going to have to make some rapid alterations to his plans. Central to all of this was a King of Cups.

We drank coffee quietly as we watched sunlight filter across the horizon; the peacefulness of the morning defied our pensive mood. As we waited for the inevitable phone call that would send him away on urgent business and me back to the airport, he asked if a King of Cups had featured in any of my readings. It was only then that the penny dropped as I recounted the details.

When the King of Cups never materialised to somehow cancel my journey, I had wrongly assumed destiny must have outplayed him somewhere along the track. Little did I realise, this unknown person was waiting at the other end to cut my visit short. Oh yes, the court cards, the heroes and the villains of the plot!

The Desire for Change
"Tread softly because you tread upon my dreams."
—W. B. Yeats

Three of the case studies featured the Tower in the wishes position of the Anchor; given our normal associations with this card, it helps to see a positive side to the interpretation when it appears in this position. This card tends to show when someone would really like a radical shake-up in their life.

It is not unusual to find the Death card here either, indicating the desire for a final ending to something considered major to them, whilst the Devil in the wishes position often signals secret plans they are formulating.

The Fool also appeared in this position twice in the case studies, revealing a desire to follow a new path, or one that may appear different and exciting from the normal lifestyle.

The card that appears in the wishes position could easily be dismissed too lightly, yet the insight it provides of the seeker's mindset can delve deeply into their desires; that which they are inwardly longing for at the present time. I wondered whether to rename this position, because "wishes" sounds flimsy in comparison to the emotions conjured by "desire"—it seems more appropriate to what people often experience with the card found here.

I have always found this card similar to opening a secret, but it has only been through recording the case studies that the position's real impact hit me on a conscious level. As I reflect upon previous readings now, I realise that in many cases the card found in this position represents the seeker's hidden motivation. Therefore something felt strongly on this level can drive their actions and ultimately shape the future outcome. Many people are most surprised by your findings when you inform them what this card reveals and discuss their thoughts and feelings surrounding the meaning with you. Since this may not be something they openly discuss with others it can be insightful to us in helping the person define, acknowledge, or attain their inner wishes, desires, and dreams. Keep in mind W. B. Yeats's famous words and tread softly, dear reader.

The Reader's Journey

With every reading our knowledge and experience grows. The insight the cards provide us with presents an unfolding story, both for the seeker and ourselves, in a never-ending journey of wonder and self-discovery from the spread we find cast before us.

Tracking the results of these case studies has been a fascinating and intriguing exploration for me in sharing the seeker's journey with them during and after their visit, witnessing the cards application to their various circumstances, the effect of their reading upon them, and watching as they made their choices with the situations life presented. It sometimes felt difficult to retain the usual professional detachment required as a reader, due to my very close observation.

Howard Beckman, Vedic astrologer and good friend, once told me, "Opportunity is brought by karma, but then it is up to you." I found myself reflecting upon those words as I watched the events of these people's lives unfolding. I feel it very well describes much of the mystery that surrounds the divination aspect of reading Tarot cards—the many questions that follow regarding fate, destiny, and free will.

The circumstances surrounding our lives are similar to an ever-changing landscape, a myriad of elements operating with mysterious synchronicity—the interconnection and relativity—each tiny detail with the potential to alter the consequences as they quietly mingle in the emerging scenery. Perhaps the only thing that changes is our awareness to the subtleties of what surrounds us, the recognition and consequent actions we take in the seemingly timeless string of moments, shaping the direction of the path we choose to follow, the infinite dance of life, and our momentary place within it.

The hour is late, or perhaps due to my nocturnal writing pattern, it is early. Daylight scatters remnants of the night into wisps of inky streamers across the North Yorkshire sky, as the dawn chorus heralds the closing sequence in my familiar pattern of sharing these moments with you. From my corner of the world to yours, all that remains is for me to wish you a safe and joyful journey.

Appendix A

Tarot Card Meanings

As this book is not aimed at beginners it is anticipated that you would have developed your own meanings for each card. However, in order to assist in showing how I came to the interpretations within the enclosed readings, this list is intended as a brief summary of keywords and associations that I use.

Themes of the Suits:

- Wands—Action and enterprise
- Cups—Emotions, love, and happiness
- Swords—Difficulty and challenges
- Pentacles—Material concerns

About Court Card Interpretations

My treatment of interpretations for the court cards is perhaps slightly different from convention. However, it is a format that works well for me in readings, and so I present it for you here as used. Individual and lengthier interpretations can be found in *Easy Tarot: Learn to Read the Cards Once and For All!*

In Considering a Medieval Royal Court

- **Pages** were often messengers. Therefore, pages represent messages, relevant to suit element—but can also be children or minors.

- **Knights** were considered gallant and noble, bold defenders of the realm, actively involved in orders from the crown, and therefore represent forms of action surrounded by high energy, relevant to the suit.
- **Kings** and **Queens** as the rulers of the kingdom were expected to be wise, mature, and responsible leaders and therefore represent adult males and females, respectively.

The natural characteristics of the pages, queens, and kings are similar and representative of their suit, excepting the variance of maturity and gender. In each section of the suit interpretations the main personality traits are shown as a group, with only some of the additional variances shown. Knights are used as events rather than people.

The Minor Arcana

Wands

- **Ace of Wands:** The start of a new enterprise, business venture, or job. A new way of life. Birth. Inspiration. Creativity. Passion. New ideas. Usually surrounded by a high degree of excitement and enthusiasm. (Pregnancy or birth when with the Empress.)
- **Two of Wands:** Ideas beginning to manifest into reality. Initial progress being made. Awareness of future choices on the path. Possibility of partnership, collaboration, or negotiations (particularly in business/enterprise).
- **Three of Wands:** First stages of success in projects; a sense of accomplishment within this. Focus and future planning.
- **Four of Wands:** Stability, harmony; a sense of contentment with self and life. Rest and relaxation after labour, perhaps a holiday or short break. Possibility of wedding plans being made.
- **Five of Wands:** Petty obstacles. Minor squabbling. Differences and conflicting opinions. Competitive forces. Power struggles. Challenges, although nothing insurmountable.
- **Six of Wands:** Efforts and achievements recognised by others. Awards and honours. Promotion. Satisfaction with accomplishments. Bearer of great news.
- **Seven of Wands:** Defending your ideals and beliefs. Having the courage of your convictions. Successfully defending your position.

- **Eight of Wands:** News coming in swiftly. Sudden activity and excitement following good news arriving. Events speeding up after a dormant period. Travel, often by air.

- **Nine of Wands:** Having courage, strength, and determination when you feel it has already been spent. Boldly protecting that which has been worked for. Not giving up on the brink of success. Perseverance.

- **Ten of Wands:** Feeling overwhelmed, weighed down, or overburdened. Carrying too many responsibilities. Look for ways to make the load lighter.

Court Cards—Wands

Natural characteristics and personality traits for Page (child or minor), Queen (adult female), King (adult male)

- Active and action-orientated, energetic, dynamic, enthusiastic, exciting, warm, cheerful, optimistic, dislikes detail—one who wants to "just get on with it." Entrepreneurial tendencies, always busy.

- Vocationally may be connected to: sales, marketing and/or advertising, promotion and development, sports, leisure, entrepreneurs. Often fast-paced environments with variety and an element of freedom or free-thinking.

- Negatively: Impulsive, rash, risk-taker, rule-breaker, quick or hot tempered, selfish, impatient, over-confident, arrogant, takes on too many things at once thus appearing chaotic or disorganised.

- May refer to astrological fire signs.

- **Page of Wands:** As messages, often connected to work or enterprise but pleasant, unless negatively aspected.

- **Knight of Wands:** Change of residence. Long journey. Brings a high degree of energy into play. (Sometimes home or property renovations.)

Cups

- **Ace of Cups:** Beginning of love and happiness. New relationships. The start of something new that brings happiness into the home for loved ones. Emotional happiness.

- **Two of Cups:** Harmonious love union. Taking a relationship to the next level. Can be reconciliation and rediscovery of an emotional bond. Usually represents romantic love.

- **Three of Cups:** Emotional happiness and abundance. Progress in a relationship. Celebrations or reasons to celebrate with others, such as engagements, weddings, anniversaries, christenings. Happy conclusion.

- **Four of Cups:** Nonchalance. Apathy. Boredom. Divine discontent. Be careful not to miss an opportunity due to feelings of indifference.

- **Five of Cups:** Loss, but something still remains. Sense of betrayal. Grieving over past actions. Regrets.

- **Six of Cups:** Something from the past returning. A "blast from the past," old love returned. Old acquaintances. Connections to childhood. Happy memories. Nostalgia.

- **Seven of Cups:** Imagination in overdrive. Indecision due to various options that seem available, although all may not be what they seem. Illusionary situations—take care in making decisions.

- **Eight of Cups:** Disillusion leads to abandonment. Walking away from a situation through choice, although usually disappointed, having heavily invested emotionally. Finally pursuing a new path.

- **Nine of Cups:** The "wish" card and its fulfilment. Abundance. Emotional and material contentment. Sensual pleasures.

- **Ten of Cups:** Committed and contented love. Marriage. Happy home life. Perfect realisation of emotional love.

Court Cards—Cups
Natural characteristics and personality traits for Page (child or minor), Queen (adult female), King (adult male)

- Kind, caring, sensitive, creative, artistic, romantic, emotional, empathic, thoughtful, gentle, easy-going nature, usually well-liked with few enemies, non-confrontational.

- Vocationally may be connected to: caring professions, medical, teaching, social work, the church, consultancy, human resources, the arts, fashion, interior design, hair and beauty.

- Negatively: dreamy, unrealistic, oversensitive, co-dependant or clingy, victim or martyr mentality, can completely withdraw and shut others out. Sugary or two-faced, may manipulate a situation rather than tackle it head-on.
  - May refer to astrological water signs.
- **Page of Cups:** As messages coming in: happy news of an emotional nature—unless badly aspected.
- **Knight of Cups:** Knights represent action. Invitations of love. Marriage proposal. Offers and proposals. (I have seen this card representing offers made in property and business.) Events bring emotional energy into play.

Swords

- **Ace of Swords:** Victory and triumph over difficulties. Provides a great force of strength and inner power with the ability to overcome adversity. Well-deserved success through one's own actions. The proverbial Ace up your sleeve.
- **Two of Swords:** Stalemate, deadlock; inertia. Indecision through confused thoughts or blocked emotions. Being of two minds over something. Mental block.
- **Three of Swords:** Quarrels. Family upheavals. Stormy emotions. Sorrow and tears. Separation (although this can be attributed to distance).
- **Four of Swords:** Period of rest and recovery after strain. Detachment from outside events. Withdrawal. Feeling a need for solitude or retreat. A period of rejuvenation to regroup resources before continuing. Recharging your batteries. Convalescence.
- **Five of Swords:** Hidden agenda with an element of deceit at play. Dishonest dealings. Underhandedness. A selfish victory that will be short-lived. Something lost in an unfair manner. Malice and spite. Watch your back. Skulduggery. Can indicate someone leaving suddenly without explanation and lack of sensitivity.
- **Six of Swords:** Moving out of stormy waters into calmer times. Matters will improve and harmony restored. A journey over water.
- **Seven of Swords:** Situations not going as anticipated. An unexpected twist. Using speech, talk, and diplomacy instead of heavy-handed methods.

- **Eight of Swords:** Feeling restricted or trapped. Mental fears creating paralysis and confusion. Mental monsters. Imprisonment.

- **Nine of Swords:** Anxiety and worrying. Anguish. Despair. Suffering. Misery. Depression. Sometimes illness.

- **Ten of Swords:** Brings an ending. Ruined or failed plans. Disappointment. Sense of loss.

Court Cards—Swords
Natural characteristics and personality traits for Page (child or minor), Queen (adult female), King (adult male)

- Agile and analytical mind. Articulate. Responsible. Independent. Strong and loyal. Honest and fair. Rational. Efficient and well-organised. Appears quite serious in nature, can seem cool and detached. Deep thinkers. Mysterious, "still waters run deep." The people's champion, or champion of the underdog, often defends those less fortunate or weaker than themselves.

- Vocationally may be connected to: law, uniforms or government, science, mathematics, engineering, information technology, detailed analytical work.

- Negatively: can be overly critical, cold or impersonal. Insensitive. Unforgiving. Ability to completely switch off emotions. Can verbally demolish people. In the extreme, cruel and bullying.

- May refer to astrological air signs.

- **Page of Swords:** As messages coming in: news that may be delayed or considered disappointing. Can represent troubles with a child or petty gossip (usually minor in nature).

- **Knight of Swords:** Brings a high degree of speed and energy into play. Situations or events can appear chaotic or confusing due to the sheer speed at which they appear and unfold.

Pentacles

- **Ace of Pentacles:** Beginning of prosperity and material gains. Important documents of material significance such as house or land deeds, bank accounts, wills, company accounts, educational awards, or travel documents. Marriage contracts—with the correct associations. Gifts of gold. Inheritance. (For writers, can represent manuscripts.)

- **Two of Pentacles:** Successfully maintaining a balance. Juggling more than one project simultaneously—home/work balance, etc. Juggling finances.

- **Three of Pentacles:** Work that you enjoy and have natural ability for. Sense of achievement in endeavours that can bring recognition. Initial stages of completion with successful attainment.

- **Four of Pentacles:** Can indicate holding back. A calculated risk needs to be taken to move the situation forward. (Be careful not to miss an opportunity due to this.) Being prepared to work hard to achieve goals.

- **Five of Pentacles:** Financial problems or anxieties. Material loss. Hardship. In a different context may also show feelings of loss on an emotional or spiritual level.

- **Six of Pentacles:** Gifts. Generosity. Sharing what one has with others. Material gains.

- **Seven of Pentacles:** Hard work and patience will be rewarded. Financial applications and sales negotiations are well aspected. Gathering in your harvest. Planning for the future—once the harvest is collected it must be replenished.

- **Eight of Pentacles:** Card of the apprentice—learning or studying new skills. New work or new job (particularly if with the Ace of Wands). Developing talents and abilities.

- **Nine of Pentacles:** Material success attained through one's own efforts. Financial independence. Material comforts. Enjoying the fruits of your labours. Feeling satisfied and content with accomplishments. Financial increase.

- **Ten of Pentacles:** Home and family stability. The family home. Material gains. Wealth and prosperity. Property sales. Inheritance. Material possessions passed down through generations. Content and stable home life.

Court Cards—Pentacles
Natural characteristics and personality traits for Page (child or minor), Queen (adult female), King (adult male)

- Patient, methodical, hard working, organised. Steadfast, dependable, practical, loyal, and reliable. Doesn't cut corners and takes care of the details. Works steadily towards goals and usually accomplishes them. Generous but not wasteful, often financially astute.

- Vocationally can be connected to: finance, property/land, food, jewels or precious metals, animals, agriculture, tradesmen. Can hold top positions or indicate one who is wealthy or financially comfortable.

- Negatively may be: extremely stubborn, inflexible, overly materialistic, or miserly.

- May refer to astrological earth signs.

- **Page of Pentacles:** As messages coming in: news of a material nature. Good news brought to you by someone that will positively affect your life (unless badly aspected).

- **Knight of Pentacles:** Finally, results are forthcoming. Represents something you have patiently waited for, or methodically worked towards, coming through at last.

The Major Arcana

- **0—The Fool:** New and unexpected situation from out of the blue requiring a major choice. New pathways that may be unfamiliar. An element of excitement and some nervous apprehension may accompany this event. A leap into the unknown.

- **I—The Magician:** Skill. Having the confidence in one's own ability, as the talents required are already possessed. Being pro-active. Focussed will and energy upon a task or skill in order to attain it.

- **II—The High Priestess:** Mysteries or secrets being revealed that will be to your benefit once known. Potential as yet unfulfilled. Listening to your intuition. Esoteric or higher studies. Can relate to caring professions rather than those of a more logical, practical nature.

- **III—The Empress:** Fruitfulness and success. Bringing things to fruition through nurturing. Motherhood or parenting. Can show with marriage cards and strengthens relationships. With Ace of Wands may indicate birth.

- **IV—The Emperor:** Leadership. Ambition. Authority. Power. The necessity for reasoning and logical thought. Material and emotional stability.

- **V—The Hierophant:** Large and structured organisations/institutions. Convention and tradition. Moral values. Traditional ways of doing things. A mentor or wise person one can consult. The Church or organized religion as a whole. Marriage.

- **VI—The Lovers:** Romantic love, and our idealised view of the perfection of this state. An important love relationship. Choices may need to be made that will affect both parties within the relationship (although not of negative connotation unless badly aspected by surrounding cards).

- **VII—The Chariot:** Triumph over difficulties but not without effort. Keeping focus in one direction and not allowing energy to become scattered. May indicate travel.

- **VIII—Strength:** The power of inner strength. Being in a strong position. Courage. The more "feminine" qualities of patience, diplomacy, and quiet determination required as opposed to aggressive tendencies to achieve the desired result. Sexual attraction and magnetism. Endurance with grace under pressure. Courage to persist and prevail in order to succeed.

- **IX—The Hermit:** Wisdom and knowledge. Accessing and listening to the inner voice of the higher self. May require solitude to think things through.

- **X—The Wheel of Fortune:** Destiny. A new cycle of luck is due to commence; a window of opportunity opening. Fate and fortune.

- **XI—Justice:** Legal matters, contracts or documents. The need for a balanced and logical mind in making decisions. Justice being served. With the Eight of Swords and the Devil, may indicate imprisonment.

- **XII—The Hanging Man:** Life in suspension. Limbo. The alternative view—thinking outside the box, lateral thinking, etc. Looking at matters from a different viewpoint in order to gain a new perspective. A sacrifice being made now in order to gain something more beneficial in the longer term. An unconventional approach.

- **XIII—Death:** The image of Death is symbolic—not literal. It heralds the ending of one phase of life to make way for a new one. It does *not* imply death in the physical sense, but represents major change and transformation.

- **XIV—Temperance:** Moderation. Harmony. Patience. Healing. Balanced emotions—or the need for. Blending opposites into a harmonious state. Can bring reconciliation.

- **XV—The Devil:** Feeling bogged down by a situation. Self-enslavement. Addiction. Obsession. Excess. Secret plans. Can show improvement in sex life.

- **XVI—The Tower:** Unexpected change, often happening swiftly. News that may bring a shock. The removal of structures falsely believed to be true. Disruptive influences, usually external.

- **XVII—The Star:** Hope for the future. Optimism and faith for brighter times ahead. Healing. Excellent card for those in the arts or entertainment industry, as it can bring public recognition.

- **XVIII—The Moon:** Fluctuating emotions. Allow time for things to become known that have not yet surfaced. Delay decision-making until more facts are known. Possible deception or illusionary situations if badly aspected.

- **XIX—The Sun**: Happiness; joy; contentment. Fulfilment. Success—personal, material, or business. Good health, or improvement. Extremely positive and auspicious card.

- **XX—Judgement:** Revival. Renewal. Something resurrected. Karmic influence—as you sow, so shall you reap. Something with roots in the past. The ability to move forward and make better choices based on past lessons learned.

- **XXI—The World:** Completion. Brings conclusion to matters. Assured success and accomplishment. The achievement of a sought-after goal. Integration and wholeness. Sometimes, to a lesser degree, international travel.

Bibliography

Bunning, Joan. *Learning Tarot Reversals.* York Beach, ME: Red Wheel/Weiser, 2003.

Boyer, Janet. *The Back in Time Tarot Book.* Charlottesville, VA: Hampton Roads Publishing Company, 2008.

Connolly, Eileen. *Tarot. A New Handbook for the Apprentice.* Hammersmith, London: Aquarian Press, 1986.

DuQuette, Lon Milo. *Understanding Aleister Crowley's Thoth Tarot.* York Beach, ME: Red Wheel/Weiser, 2003.

Ellershaw, Josephine, and Ciro Marchetti. *Easy Tarot: Learn to Read the Cards Once and For All!* Woodbury, MN: Llewellyn Publications, 2007.

Giblin, Les. *Skill With People.* ISBN 0-9616416-0-6. 1968, 1972, 1985. (No publisher given)

Greer, Mary. *Book of Tarot Reversals.* St. Paul, MN: Llewellyn Publications, 2002.

———. *Tarot for Your Self.* Franklin Lakes, NJ: New Page Books. 2002.

Kaplan, S.R. *Tarot Cards for Fun and Fortune Telling.* New York: US Games Systems Inc., 1970.

Marchetti, Ciro, and Barbara Moore. *The Gilded Tarot.* St. Paul, MN: Llewellyn Publications, 2004.

Pollack, Rachel. *Tarot Wisdom: Spiritual Teachings and Deeper Meanings.* Woodbury, MN: Llewellyn Publications, 2008.

Waite, Arthur Edward. *The Pictorial Key to the Tarot.* Reprint. Stamford, CT: US Games Systems Inc. 2003.

Yeats, W. B. *The Wind Among the Reeds.* New York: J. Lane, The Bodley Head, 1899.

Tarot Card Key

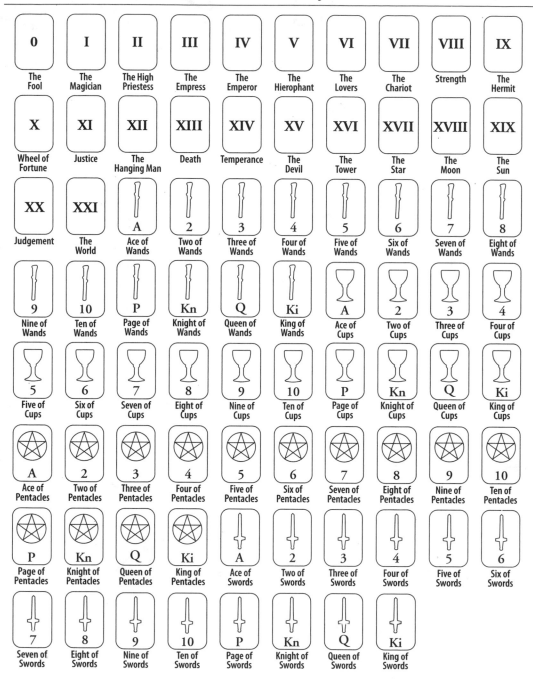

0 The Fool	**I** The Magician	**II** The High Priestess
III The Empress	**IV** The Emperor	**V** The Hierophant
VI The Lovers	**VII** The Chariot	**VIII** Strength
IX The Hermit	**X** Wheel of Fortune	**XI** Justice
XII The Hanging Man	**XIII** Death	**XIV** Temperance
XV The Devil	**XVI** The Tower	**XVII** The Star
XVIII The Moon	**XIX** The Sun	**XX** Judgement
XXI The World		

Wands:
A Ace of Wands, 2 Two of Wands, 3 Three of Wands, 4 Four of Wands, 5 Five of Wands, 6 Six of Wands, 7 Seven of Wands, 8 Eight of Wands, 9 Nine of Wands, 10 Ten of Wands, P Page of Wands, Kn Knight of Wands, Q Queen of Wands, Ki King of Wands

Cups:
A Ace of Cups, 2 Two of Cups, 3 Three of Cups, 4 Four of Cups, 5 Five of Cups, 6 Six of Cups, 7 Seven of Cups, 8 Eight of Cups, 9 Nine of Cups, 10 Ten of Cups, P Page of Cups, Kn Knight of Cups, Q Queen of Cups, Ki King of Cups

Pentacles:
A Ace of Pentacles, 2 Two of Pentacles, 3 Three of Pentacles, 4 Four of Pentacles, 5 Five of Pentacles, 6 Six of Pentacles, 7 Seven of Pentacles, 8 Eight of Pentacles, 9 Nine of Pentacles, 10 Ten of Pentacles, P Page of Pentacles, Kn Knight of Pentacles, Q Queen of Pentacles, Ki King of Pentacles

Swords:
A Ace of Swords, 2 Two of Swords, 3 Three of Swords, 4 Four of Swords, 5 Five of Swords, 6 Six of Swords, 7 Seven of Swords, 8 Eight of Swords, 9 Nine of Swords, 10 Ten of Swords, P Page of Swords, Kn Knight of Swords, Q Queen of Swords, Ki King of Swords